Harry Potter Places Book Four

NEWTs: Northeastern England Wizarding Treks

A Novel Holiday Travel Guidebook

By CD Miller

Harry Potter Places BOOK FOUR
NEWTs: Northeastern England Wizarding Treks
A Novel Holiday Travel Guidebook

by CD Miller

Published by:
A Novel Holiday Travel Guidebooks
16614 226th Street
Ashland, NE 68003
http://www.anovelholiday.com

All rights reserved. No part of this book may be reproduced or transmitted in any form or by any means, electronic or mechanical—including photocopying, recording, or any information storage and retrieval system—without written permission from the author, except for the inclusion of brief quotations in a review.

The publisher and author(s) of *Harry Potter Places* Book Four have taken great care to ensure that all information provided is correct and accurate at the time of manuscript submission. However, errors and omissions—whether typographical, clerical or otherwise—do sometimes occur, and may occur anywhere within the body of this publication.

Changes in real-life site information will inevitably occur. As aptly stated by the Internationally-renown travel guidebook author, **Rick Steves**: "Guidebooks begin to yellow even before they're printed." This rule holds true for eBooks, as well.

Users of any *Harry Potter Places* travel guidebook are advised to access the Internet links provided within each Site entry in order to obtain the most up-to-date information during the planning of your UK Potter holiday. For instance, the ticket and entry fees cited are those that were in effect during our last pass at researching each site.

Currency equivalents are offered only to provide an *approximate idea* of what British Pounds (£) equals in US Dollars ($). Currency exchange rates change daily. Check current foreign exchange rates by using a free Internet currency converter such as the one offered by **Oanda**:
http://www.oanda.com/currency/converter/

The publisher and author(s) of *Harry Potter Places* travel guidebooks disclaim any liability to any party for loss, injury, or damage incurred as a direct or indirect consequence of errors, omissions, or post-manuscript-submission information changes, whether such errors, omissions, or changes result from negligence, accident, or any other cause.

Copyright © 2012 by Charly D Miller
A Novel Holiday Travel Guidebooks Publishing Company
Printed in the United States of America
ISBN 978-1-938285-19-6

Publisher's Cataloging-in-Publication Data
Miller, Charly D, 1956 -
Harry Potter Places Book Four (Color)—NEWTs: Northeastern England Wizarding Treks
by Charly D Miller.
    p. cm.
    1. Travel Guides—United Kingdom—.
    ISBN 978-1-938285-19-6   (softbound) $29.95
I. Title.
DA650.H75 M460 2012

Disclaimers

J.K. Rowling's *Harry Potter* books are so popular, that an amazing number of **unauthorized** *Harry Potter* guidebooks have been published over the years.
http://harrypotter.wikia.com/wiki/List_of_Harry_Potter_unofficial_guidebooks

In order to avoid the threat of litigation related to copyright or trademark infringement, all unauthorized *Harry Potter* guidebooks publish at least one **Disclaimer**. Below are the **several** important *Harry Potter Places* Disclaimers.

An Unauthorized *Harry Potter* Travel Guidebook

Harry Potter Places Book Four [hereinafter referred to as **HPP Book Four**] is not authorized, approved, endorsed, nor licensed by J.K. Rowling [hereinafter referred to as **JKR**], Warner Bros. Entertainment, Inc. [hereinafter referred to as **WB Inc**], the Scholastic Corporation, Raincoast Books, Bloomsbury Publishing Plc., nor by any other persons, entities, corporations or companies claiming a proprietary interest in the *Harry Potter* books, movies, or related merchandise.

HPP Book Four is not officially associated with the seven *Harry Potter* novels written and copyrighted by JKR. Nor is HPP Book Four in any way officially associated with the eight *Harry Potter* movies produced and trademarked by WB Inc.

The Purpose of HPP Book Four

HPP Book Four is written solely for the purpose of providing an historical review of, and directions for finding, the **real-life** Northeastern England locations that:
- Were mentioned within one or more of the *Harry Potter* novels.
- Are sites where Harry Potter filming took place.
- Significantly influenced the design of studio sets built for filming one or more of the *Harry Potter* movies.

HP-Associated Names, Places, Titles or Terminology

HPP Book Four does not claim, nor does it intend to imply, ownership of, or proprietary rights to, any of the fictional character or place names mentioned within JKR's *Harry Potter* novels, nor any of the titles or terminology used or created by JKR within her books or within the movies made thereof.

Harry Potter Places Book Four

More information about Potter and Potterlike terminology found within HPP Book Four is provided in the **Prior Incantato** section.

Publication of *Harry Potter* Movie Screenshots

Screenshots are split-second still photos captured from a movie. Each of the HPP Book Four Potter Site entries include one or more small movie screenshots. The sole purpose of including them is to enhance the experience of *Harry Potter* fans [**Potterites**] who visit a real-life film site, or a real-life place that strongly influenced movie studio set design. By having one or more screenshots to observe while visiting, Potterites are better able to recognize the specific areas where filming occurred, and are armed with a guide important to assuming positions similar to that of the actors in the scene(s) filmed at the site when snapping their personal photographs.

To be an effective site identification and photography guide, however, *Harry Potter* movie screenshots had to be substantially *altered* in a variety of ways so that the site location's **background** could more easily be recognized.

All eight *Harry Potter* films were produced and trademarked by WB Inc. HPP Book Four does not claim, nor does it intend to imply, ownership of, or proprietary rights to, any portions of the *Harry Potter* movies. The caption of every screenshot and screenshot segment that appears within HPP should read "™©WB Inc." Because this info is given here, we instead have captioned HPP screenshots with identification of the movie from which it was captured.

Use of Google Maps UK Images to Create Potter Maps

In order to assist visiting Potterites to find multiple filming locations within one Site (such as the Knight Bus Pickup Playground, or the Ministry of Magic Area), a few **Potter Maps** were created for *Harry Potter Places* Book Four.

When using Google Maps UK images to create Potter Maps, HPP Book Four authors strictly adhered to the *Google Maps and Google Earth Content Rules & Guidelines*, and appropriately attributed Google with credit for the full-sized Potter Map included within a Supplementum PDF posted on the Internet, as well as for any thumbnail-sized Potter Map images published within the travel guidebook.

HPP Book Three does not claim, nor does it intend to imply, ownership of, or proprietary rights to, any of the Google Maps UK images used within the travel guidebook or the Supplementum PDFs posted on HarryPotterPlaces.com.

Author vs Authors of *Harry Potter Places*

The **A Novel Holiday** travel guidebook publishing company concept was solely conceived by Ms. Charly D Miller in 2007, as was the concept of the first

Disclaimers

series of A Novel Holiday (**ANH**) travel guidebooks, **Harry Potter Places**. However, during the researching and writing of HPP travel guidebooks (as well as during design of the ANH and HPP websites), Ms. Miller was so generously assisted by other individuals, that she feels unworthy of claiming sole credit for authoring the text's or websites' content. Thus, **plural terms**—such as, "authors" … "we" … "our"—are used throughout the HPP travel guidebooks, as well as throughout the ANH and HPP websites, when referring to the writers or creators of same.

However, for all legal purposes, every A Novel Holiday *Harry Potter Places* travel guidebook was solely written and published by CD Miller. She, alone, is responsible for all the content ultimately published within any eBook or print versions of the HPP travel guidebooks, as well as all the content posted on ANH and HPP websites.

Ms. Charly D Miller hereby avows and affirms that any and all other individuals who participated in or contributed to the researching, writing, or publication of *Harry Potter Places* travel guidebooks and associated websites, are **indemnified and held harmless** from and against: any and all demands, claims, and damages to persons or property, losses and liabilities, including attorney's fees arising out of or caused by any form of litigation brought against the A Novel Holiday *Harry Potter Places* travel guidebooks or websites.

Harry Potter Places Book Four

Credits and Acknowledgments

Thank you, Tara and Wolfgang!

The two most generous and dedicated Contributing *Harry Potter Places* Researchers are Ms. Tara Bellers of the US, and Mr. Wolfgang Mletzko of Germany.

Tara Bellers traveled from the US to the UK on three different occasions between 2009 and 2011. During each of those trips, she voluntarily spent personal time investigating answers to Potter Place questions that couldn't be found on the Internet. In addition to snapping location pix for us, Tara discovered and reported info important to enhancing other Potterites' enjoyment of a similar visit.

When not traveling, Tara continued to significantly contribute to this project. While at home, she independently performed hundreds of hours of Internet research, leading to the discovery of several important Potter Places we might have missed. Thanks to Tara, Potterites will have no trouble finding even the most obscure UK Potter Places.

Wolfgang Mletzko began visiting UK Potter Places long before A Novel Holiday travel guidebooks (let alone *Harry Potter Places*) were even a concept. Since 2002, Wolfgang has performed several well-researched UK Potter treks, and always has freely-posted his marvelous photos and Potter travel tips on his website—which is how we found him!
http://www.bdyg.homepage.t-online.de/index.html

If you can't read German, go to **Google's Translation** website and paste-in Wolfgang's website address.
http://translate.google.com/

Special Mention

Thank you to **Keith and Sandra Simmonds of the Glendale House in Goathland**, for all your kind assistance—even though we'd not stayed in your B&B.

Photo Credits

Beneath each photograph in *Harry Potter Places* is the name of the person who snapped the pic. With few exceptions, permission for using these photos was granted free of charge. Some photos were obtained from **Wikipedia** or **Wikimedia**, where they were posted by photographers who generously offered the freedom of their commercial re-use.

Art Credit

The *Harry Potter Places* **Coat of Arms**—an emblem seen on the title page of every *Harry Potter Places* Supplementum and Portkey PDF, as well as in the Banner atop each HarryPotterPlaces.com webpage—was designed by two terrifically talented graphic artists, newly-weds **Karen Dale** and **Ben Dale**. They also created our three site ratings icons. Thank you both, so very much, for all your work!

http://www.coroflot.com/kstoehr
http://bendale.daportfolio.com/

Book Cover Credits

DC Carson created all five of the original 2012 HPP Book Covers—free of charge! Were it not for her, the HPP website would not have had images to use while CD Miller was still broke.

All photos used for the HPP Book Covers were snapped by **Ms. Tara Bellers**.

From the Author, CD Miller

To Ms. Carson

I am more grateful to Ms. Carson than mere words can possibly convey. Dina has helped me with this project from the very beginning—for more

Acknowledgments

than three years—entirely free of charge! These guidebooks would be *krappe* were it not for Dina's incredible writing talent and editing instruction, as well as her invaluable assistance with getting the eBook and print versions published. Dina also was vitally important to the design of the A Novel Holiday and *Harry Potter Places* websites.

My fondest wish is to someday be able to reciprocate, and help her as significantly as she's helped me. Unfortunately, I cannot imagine what *I* could ever do that Dina can't do better! Thankfully, I anticipate being able to *financially* reward her for all her work very soon.

Then, there's Tara Bellers

I couldn't afford to visit the UK more than *once*—a measly 2 weeks in 2008—while initially working on the *Harry Potter Places* project. Thus, the information offered in all HPP Books would be terrifically incomplete were it not for Tara's **voluntary** UK Potter Place site research and photography, as well as the Internet research she continues to freely perform. In addition to that, Tara took me to the *Wizarding World of Harry Potter* in Orlando, Florida, in 2010!

I'll *never* be able to adequately thank Tara for all her generosity and assistance. But, perhaps I'll soon be able to reward her by taking her on an all-expenses-paid UK trip!

As for my Personal Friends

Susan and Bob, Jamie, Janet, Chet, Sandy, Leeenda and Mike ... these are just a *few* of the scores of people I need to thank!

I was broke and homeless. (Much like JKR was while writing *Sorcerer's Stone*, oddly enough.) Yet, each of my friends contributed—in their own way—to ensure that I had a place to live, and the means for living comfortably, during the several years it took me to complete my first HPP travel guidebooks. You guys have no idea how much I've appreciated your help. I swear that, someday, I'll find a way of repaying you.

Lastly, to Drew and Annabeth, Auntie Dot and Uncle Itchy

Bless You for always believing in me!

Harry Potter Places Book Four

TABLE OF CONTENTS

Title Page and Copyright Information	i
Disclaimers	iii
Credits and Acknowledgements	vii
Table of Contents	xi

Chapter 1—PRIOR INCANTATO (Introduction)

Harry Potter Places Portkeys … 1

😊 😐 ☹ Ratings Icon Guide

The Potterite Prime Directive

Harry Potter Places Terminology

Chapter 2—LUMOS BRITANNIA

Non-Potter UK Travel Guidebooks	7
Free UK Travel Tips Available on the Internet	
Official UK Travel Internet Websites	
UK VAT Tax Information	
Potterite UK Travel Supplementums	

Chapter 3—LUMOS NEWTs

Northeastern England Wizarding Treks	13

POTTER PLACES in NORTHEASTERN ENGLAND

Please Note: Our Site numbers continue from *Harry Potter Places* Book Three—Snitch-Seeking in Southern England and Wales.

Chapter 4—Site #44: **Alnwick Castle:** Alnwick, Northumberland	15
Chapter 5—Site #45: **Durham Cathedral:** Durham, County Durham	37

Harry Potter Places Book Four

Chapter 6 — Site #46: **Goathland Railway Station:** 55
Goathland, North Yorkshire

Chapter 7 — Site #47: **Hardwick Hall:** Chesterfield, Derbyshire 71

Chapter 8 — Site #48: **Malham Cove Limestone Pavement:** 85
Malham, North Yorkshire

Chapter 9 — Site #49: **National Railway Museum:** 103
Yorkshire *or* County Durham

Index 113

Prior Incantato

Welcome to the **A Novel Holiday** travel guidebook, ***Harry Potter Places* Book Four—NEWTs: Northeastern England Wizarding Treks**, the fourth of five guidebooks designed to help *Harry Potter* Fans (**Potterites**) visit places found in the United Kingdom of Great Britain (the **UK**) associated with the *Harry Potter* Universe (the **Potterverse**). In the Potterverse, you'll find:
- Real-life places mentioned within J.K. Rowling's *Harry Potter* novels.
- Real-life locations where *Harry Potter* movie filming took place.
- Real-life sites that significantly influenced *Harry Potter* movie studio set design.

The **Prior Incantato** section is the *Harry Potter Places* Travel Guidebook Introduction. As such, it contains important explanations of the symbols and terminology found within each of the five *Harry Potter Places* (**HPP**) travel guidebooks.

Harry Potter Places Portkeys

To assist Potterites using eBook-reading devices that don't have a web browser—devices from which you cannot apparate—or Potterites using a printed HPP travel guidebook, we've created **HPP Portkeys**: Internet-posted PDFs containing all the Internet resource links provided in each section of every HPP book.

Go to **HarryPotterPlaces.com.** Click on the link for **Book Four**, then click on the **Supplementums** link. There you can access the Portkeys.

Harry Potter Places Ratings Icon Guide

It took more than three years of research, but we managed to find *sixty-eight* (68) **Potter Places in the UK**—specifically on the island of Great Britain. However, not all of these sites are places every Potterite will enjoy. Thus, we assessed each for their reasonable importance to an average Potterite's UK holiday, and created icons that provide an *at-a-glance* recognition of their rating.

😎 The **Great Site** icon indicates a Potter Place you don't want to miss. These are important sites mentioned in the books, or film locations readily recognized in real-life.

Harry Potter Places Book Four

😊 The **Might Be Fun** icon identifies places some Potterites might find disinteresting, *or* unworthy of the inconvenience required to reach them. Each Might-Be-Fun Site's entry explains why it received that rating.

☹️ The **Skip It** icon is assigned to places we strongly suggest you *avoid* visiting, and the Site's entry explains why. Although we provide SatNav/GPS coordinates and/or addresses for Skip-It-rated sites, we do not provide directions for finding them, nor are Skip-It sites included in *any* of the suggested *Harry Potter Places* itineraries. Potterites divinely inspired to visit any Skip-It site should investigate the location using the information provided in its Site entry, then create their own itineraries.

The Potterite Prime Directive

> To **POLITELY** Go Where Potterites Need to Go
> — without **PERTURBING** anybody —
> So That Other Potterites Can *Continue*
> to ENJOY GOING THERE!

It is vitally important that all Potterites be as polite as possible when visiting *any* Potter Place. This rule is even more important when visiting a Site situated within a **private Muggle neighborhood**. It only takes *one* noisy or disrespectful fan to ruin the reception experienced by *all* Potterites who visit thereafter. Please be the very best **Potterite Ambassador** you can possibly be, everywhere you go.

Terminology Used within *Harry Potter Places*

Like any other author of fiction, J.K. Rowling (**JKR**) exercised *artistic license* when selecting or creating names, phrases, and terms for her Potterverse. Most often, she borrowed from Latin and Greek languages or mythologies. Occasionally, JKR's Potterverse terminology was influenced by other languages, such as French, Irish, Italian—even Arabic. Below is a resource link that discusses the origin of Potterverse names, phrases, and terms.
http://www.languagerealm.com/hplang/harrypotterlanguage.php

Another origin of Potterverse names, phrases, and terms reference link was offered in Harry Potter Places Books One, Two, and Three:
http://www.harrypotterfanzone.com/word-origins/

Unfortunately, the Harry Potter Fan Zone has recently disapparated from the Internet! Thanks to the WayBack Machine website, we found that now-defunct HPFZ page, and created a PDF file of it:
http://www.HarryPotterPlaces.com/DefunctWordOriginsHPFZpage.pdf

Prior Incantato

JKR also often used words that *predate* her creation of the Potterverse, such as Witch, Wizard, broomstick, and the like. Sometimes, JKR altered the previously-popular meaning of the words she used. For instance, *Time Magazine* reported in 1931 that "Muggle" was one of several slang names for a **marijuana cigarette**.

Please Note: As of 2012, the 1931 Time Magazine "Muggle" article link offered in the Prior Incantato sections of Harry Potter Places Books One through Three has been blocked from public access, unless you subscribe to Time Magazine. Thanks again to the WayBack Machine website, we found a pre-blocked copy of that article and created a PDF file of it:
http://www.HarryPotterPlaces.com/1931TimeMugglesArticle.pdf

The authors of *Harry Potter Places* have similarly exercised artistic license when using Potterverse terminology within our travel guidebooks. Some names, phrases, and terms used within HPP have the same meaning as they do in the Potterverse. Others have been redefined.

For example: **Prior Incantato** is a Potterverse incantation spoken to reveal the last spell performed by a wand. JKR created this phrase from the Latin word, *prior*, meaning former or previous, in combination with *incanto*, meaning "to enchant," or *incantate*, meaning "to speak a spell." However, in the *Harry Potter Places* travel guidebooks, Prior Incantato is the title of each books' **Introduction**.

Potterverse names, phrases, and terms found within *Harry Potter Places* that may have been independently-created by J.K. Rowling are used only for the purpose of enhancing Potterites' enjoyment of the travel guidebook. The authors of *Harry Potter Places* do not claim, nor intend to imply, ownership of, or proprietary rights to, any terminology found exclusively within *Harry Potter* books.

Some Potterverse—and Potterlike—Terms Used

Ambulatus

Although **Ambulatus** *sounds* Potterlike, it isn't found anywhere within JKR's Potterverse. Ambulate is an English word derived from Latin origins, and means, "to walk from place to place" or "move about." The Latin word for navigated, traveled, or traversed, is *ambulatus*. Ambulatus is used in the title of *Harry Potter Places* sections that provide directions for walking or traveling about within the cities of Oxford and Edinburgh. (London's between-Potter-Places travel directions are found at the end of each site.)

Huffandpuff

Hufflepuff is one of the four Houses of Hogwarts School of Witchcraft and Wizardry. While **Huffandpuff** sounds like Hufflepuff, it is a term created

Harry Potter Places Book Four

by *Harry Potter Places* authors for use as the title of any particularly arduous itinerary or walking route—indicating that you may be *huffing and puffing* when you reach the end!

Lumos

In the Potterverse, Lumos is the spell-word uttered to cause a wand to emit light from its tip. Lumos is related to *lumen*, a Latin word for light. In *Harry Potter Places*, **Lumos** is used in the title of sections that *shed a light on* a particular location, providing Potter- and Non-Potter-related information important to planning or enjoying your trek to that place.

Muggle

Every Potterite knows the Potterverse definition of a Muggle. In *Harry Potter Places*, **Muggle** is a term used when referring to any Non-Potterites one might encounter while visiting a Potter place, particularly *indigenous* Non-Potterites—those who live in the private neighborhoods that Potterites may be visiting.

NEWTs

NEWTs is a Potterverse acronym for the **Nastily Exhausting Wizarding Tests** that Hogwarts' students must pass at the end of their seventh year of school. In *Harry Potter Places*, however, **NEWTs** refers to **Northeastern England Wizarding Treks**, Potter Places that can be visited in Northeastern England.

OWLs

In the Potterverse, Hogwarts' students are subjected to **OWLs—Ordinary Wizarding Level** examinations—at the end of their fifth year of school. In *Harry Potter Places*, **OWLs** stands for **Oxford Wizarding Locations**, Potter Places found in the city of Oxford.

Parseltongue Pointers

Parseltongue is the Potterverse language spoken by a Parselmouth—someone who can communicate with snakes. In *Harry Potter Places*, **Parseltongue Pointers** are guides to correctly pronouncing place names associated with UK Potter Sites.

Specialis Revelio

A Potterverse spell invoked to reveal the ingredients of a potion or the enchantments placed upon an object, **Specialis Revelio** is a phrase created from the Latin terms *specialis*, meaning special, and *revelo*, meaning "to unveil." In *Harry Potter Places*, **Specialis Revelio** is used as the title of a

Prior Incantato

section that reveals special information about visiting a particular location—including suggested itineraries.

Supplementum(s)

Another term that *sounds* Potterlike, but isn't found anywhere within JKR's Potterverse, **Supplementum** is a *Harry Potter Places* term for an Internet-posted PDF that contains extra information related to an individual Potter place. HPP Supplementums are intended to enrich a Potterite's visit to the Site they are associated with.

Please Note: Although it is more grammatically-correct to consider **Supplementum** as *both* the singular and plural version of this term, the authors of *Harry Potter Places* have elected to use **Supplementums** as the plural form of Supplementum.

Philosopher's Stone vs Sorcerer's Stone

There are a number of unconfirmed theories as to why the title of J.K. Rowling's first book, ***Harry Potter and the Philosopher's Stone***, was changed to ***Harry Potter and the Sorcerer's Stone*** for release in the USA and elsewhere. Because the authors of *Harry Potter Places* live in the USA, *Sorcerer's Stone* is used whenever we refer to the first *Harry Potter* book and movie.

We intend no disrespect to JKR—nor to Potterites living in the UK, Canada, or Australia (countries where both the book and movie are called, *Philosopher's Stone*)—by electing to use *Sorcerer's Stone* when referring to the first *Harry Potter* book and movie.

Harry Potter Places Book Four

Lumos Britannia

Lumos Britannia provides general tips for Potterites planning a visit to **the United Kingdom of Great Britain**—aka **Britannia**, aka **the UK**.

UK Travel Guidebooks

Consider purchasing one or more Non-Potter (Muggle) UK travel guidebooks related to the areas where you'll be Pottering. If your holiday is solely Potter-centric, a UK Muggle travel guidebook is *not* necessary— *Harry Potter Places* will take care of you. However, Potterites also interested in visiting Non-Potter UK places will benefit from buying one *or more* Muggle travel guidebooks.

The *Harry Potter Places* Travel Store offers links to many of the Travel Guidebooks mentioned below, including several eBook versions.

HPP Recommends Rick Steves' Guidebooks
http://www.ricksteves.com

Rick Steves has been researching and writing truly excellent travel guidebooks for over 20 years, and he publishes three frequently-updated UK guides for the places you might be traveling to. Potterites only visiting London should buy *Rick Steves' London*. If you'll be visiting London and Oxford (and/or other places in England), purchase *Rick Steves' England*. If you'll be visiting England, Wales, *and* Scotland, buy *Rick Steves' Great Britain*.

Other Popular UK Muggle Travel Guidebook Companies

Fodor's Travel Guides
http://www.fodors.com

Frommer's Travel Guides
http://www.frommers.com/

Lonely Planet Guides
http://www.lonelyplanet.com/

Rough Guides
http://www.roughguides.com/

FREE UK Travel Tips Available on the Internet

Here are our favorites.

Rick Steves' Website

Whether or not you purchase a Rick Steves travel guidebook, his website offers free access to a ton of terrific European travel tip articles: packing, safety issues, health information, communicating [phone info], money matters, and other important subjects.
http://www.ricksteves.com/plan/tips/tips_menu.htm

Steves' Website also offers free travel tip articles for visiting London, England, Wales, Edinburgh, and Scotland.
http://www.ricksteves.com/plan/destinations/britain/brit_menu.htm

Reid Bramblett's Website
http://www.reidsguides.com/

In 1997, travel expert and guidebook author Reid Bramblett began what has become one of the most helpful travel planning websites on the Internet.

> "ReidsGuides.com is focused on European trip planning, with emphasis on money-saving tips and alternatives to traditional travel techniques, such as lodging options beyond hotels, no-frills airlines, short-term car leases, and sightseeing for free."

Bramblett also offers free articles about all the **traditional** UK trip planning subjects. But, he excels at making complicated money issues easy to understand. *All* of Bramblett's money articles are valuable when planning a UK trip, particularly the ones about changing money, using credit cards, and traveler's checks.

> "Here's how to get money during your [UK] travels, strategies for getting the best deals on exchange rates, how to avoid scams and rip-offs, and ways to save money every step of the way on your vacation."

http://www.reidsguides.com/t_mo/t_mo_money.html

Visit Travel Websites Related to Planning a UK Holiday
US Department of State, Bureau of Consular Affairs' Website
http://travel.state.gov/travel/cis_pa_tw/cis/cis_1052.html

Subjects include:
   Entry/exit requirements for US citizens
   Contact information for the **US Embassy in London** and the **US Consulate in Edinburgh**.
   Medical facilities and health information

Lumos Britannia

Medical insurance
The **Smart traveler enrollment program** (STEP)
Traffic safety and road conditions

The Smart Traveler Enrollment Program (STEP) is Interesting
https://travelregistration.state.gov/ibrs/ui/

STEP is a free service provided by the US Government to US citizens who are traveling to a foreign country. By registering information about your upcoming trip abroad with STEP, the US Department of State will be able to assist you better if you experience an emergency while in the UK. It also will be able to help friends and family to get in touch with you in the event of an emergency in the US.

Potterites living in countries other than the US should explore their government's website to obtain similar international travel information and assistance.

Visit Britain Website
http://www.visitbritain.com/en/US/

Click on **Travel Tips** to reach **Customs and Immigration** information about passports and visas.
http://www.visitbritain.com/en/Travel-tips/Customs-and-immigration/

Then, click on **Traveller Tips** for links to several other important subjects.
http://www.visitbritain.com/en/Travel-tips/Traveller-tips/

Links found on Visit Britain's Traveller Tips directory page include:
  Cost of daily items & tipping information
  Free guides for your mobile [cell phone]
  Medical & health information
  Money & currency
  Public holidays & time zones
  Safety & security
  Utilities, weights & measures

Learn About the VAT Tax Before Visiting the UK

When you pay for something in the UK, there often is a **Value Added Tax** (VAT) *included* in the purchase price. The UK VAT is **20%** of the item's commercial value *before* the tax is added—a considerable amount of additional cost.

Business Travelers are the only persons who can recover the UK VAT paid on expenses such as accommodations, car rentals, petrol, and meals.

However, persons traveling to the UK for **pleasure** *can* obtain a full refund of the VAT they pay on purchases of goods such as souvenirs, clothing, leather products, and the like—but only when your total purchase at an individual store equals or exceeds £30 ($48), and only if you follow the steps necessary to reclaiming the VAT paid.

The Official British Revenue & Customs VAT Webpage
http://www.hmrc.gov.uk/vat/index.htm

The Official European VAT Webpage
http://www.brvat.com/faq/index.htm

Both of these sites provide extensive information about the UK's VAT system. Unfortunately, much of the information offered is confusing.

Reid Bramblett's *"Getting the VAT Back"* Article
Mr. Bramblett provides a **clear and simple explanation of the UK VAT system**, as well as the best tips for obtaining a VAT refund.
http://www.reidsguides.com/t_mo/t_mo_vat.html

VAT Tip Highlights:
- Every time your total purchase at an individual store equals or exceeds £30, ask the sales clerk for the form needed in order to obtain a VAT refund. Sometimes, the clerk will fill it out for you. Otherwise, be sure that **you** fill out each form at the end of the purchase day—*before* your goodies get distributed throughout your luggage.

- Attach each completed VAT form to its corresponding sales receipt.

- Stash your VAT-attached sales receipts in a single envelope or Zip-bag, so that all your VAT documents are easy to present at the airport's Customs Office when you're ready to go home.

- **When leaving the UK, visit the airport's Customs Office *before* you check your luggage!** Although it rarely happens, a Customs Officer may ask to inspect your purchases when examining your sales receipts and VAT forms. If you've already checked the bag(s) containing your purchases, your VAT reclaim forms may be denied.

Peruse the Potterite UK Travel Supplementums

Harry Potter Places **Supplementums** are PDFs freely posted on the Internet, for the benefit of any Potterite planning a UK trip.

Pre-Trip Potter Preparation
http://HarryPotterPlaces.com/tips/PreTripPrep.pdf

Lumos Britannia

Tips for refreshing your Potterverse knowledge before you leave (loading your Pensieve!) — such as enjoying a Potter Film Festival with your friends.

Packing Pointers
http://HarryPotterPlaces.com/tips/PackingPointers.pdf

General UK packing tips, including important methods of baggage identification and travel document copy storage, as well as *vital* personal supplies you'll not want to forget.

Supplies to Purchase *in* the UK
http://HarryPotterPlaces.com/tips/UKtripSupplies.pdf

Stuff you don't need to lug along while traveling to Great Britain, and where to cheaply purchase these items after you arrive.

UK Car Rental and Driving Tips
http://HarryPotterPlaces.com/tips/UKcarRental.pdf

Important considerations for selecting your rental car and preparing to drive in the UK.

UK Telephones
http://HarryPotterPlaces.com/tips/UKphones.pdf

How to dial from outside or inside the UK, and phone options available.

UK Internet Access
http://HarryPotterPlaces.com/tips/UKinternetAccess.pdf

The many options for connecting with the World Wide Web while in the UK, and what services to avoid.

UK Photography Issues
http://HarryPotterPlaces.com/tips/UKphotography.pdf

Railway station photography rules, the value of packing a cheap or disposable camera, and more.

UK Terminology Guide
http://HarryPotterPlaces.com/tips/UKterminology.pdf

A translation of UK English terms that have meanings *different* from US English terms.

Harry Potter Places Book Four

LUMOS NORTHEASTERN ENGLAND WIZARDING TREKS

The fourth *Harry Potter Places* travel guidebook, NEWTs: Northeastern England Wizarding Treks, explores **six** Potter Places located in—you guessed it—Northeastern England.

Three NEWTs are Great-Site-rated

😎 **Site #44: Alnwick Castle:** Alnwick, Northumberland

😎 **Site #45: Durham Cathedral:** Durham, County Durham

😎 **Site #46: Goathland Railway Station:** Goathland, North Yorkshire

Three NEWTs are Might-Be-Fun-rated

😐 **Site #47: Hardwick Hall:** Chesterfield, Derbyshire

😐 **Site #48: Malham Cove Limestone Pavement:** Malham, North Yorkshire

😐 **Site #49: National Railway Museum**, Yorkshire *or* County Durham

The primary difference between Great-Site- and Might-Be-Fun-rated NEWTs is whether or not they are quick and convenient to reach. Thus, **Potterites with plenty of holiday time** can consider **all NEWTs** to be **Great-Site-rated Potter Places**!

If You Visit Only *One*, it Must be Alnwick Castle (Site #44)

No other film site in all of the United Kingdom has so enthusiastically embraced and accommodated Harry Potter fans. In addition to plenty of Potter-Specific and Potter-Related tours, activities and exhibits, Alnwick Castle offers a multitude of interesting Non-Potter events and performances. Furthermore, enjoyment of **all** these tours, activities and exhibits, events and performers, are *included* in the Alnwick Castle admission fee.

Harry Potter Places Book Four

Going to the Northeastern England Wizarding Trek Sites

Each of our NEWT Site Entries provide all the information needed to make your holiday itinerary decisions *and* plot your course to the Harry Potter Places you plan to visit.

Visit the Harry Potter Places website to learn more about *Harry Potter Places* travel guidebooks, access the FREE Potterite UK Travel Supplementums we've posted, and see the **Table of Contents for all five *Harry Potter Places* travel guidebooks.**
www.HarryPotterPlaces.com

ALNWICK CASTLE

Sorcerer's Stone and Chamber of Secrets Film Sites
http://www.alnwickcastle.com
http://en.wikipedia.org/wiki/Alnwick_Castle

Google Maps UK: Alnwick Castle, Alnwick, Northumberland NE66 1NQ

SatNav/GPS coordinates and Parking Tips are provided in the **Driving to Alnwick Castle** section.

Operation Hours: Open daily from 10am to 6pm in the spring and summer (between March 31st and September 30th, 2012).
   Please Note: The Castle *occasionally* closes for administrative reasons or special events. Consult Alnwick Castle's website to check opening times during your holiday dates.

Entry Fee: Adults £14.00 ($23), Seniors £12.60 ($20), Children 5-16 years old £7.00 ($11), under-5 years old free. If you purchase tickets online, you'll receive a 5% discount.

Visit Time: Enjoying Alnwick Castle's film sites, tours, activities, exhibits, performances or events, **could easily fill an entire day**—especially when accompanied by children, or if you're also a garden fan. Schedule a *minimum* of 2 hours to visit the Gift Shop and the five Harry Potter film sites. Add an additional 45 to 60 minutes for *each* of the Alnwick Castle tours, activities, exhibits, or events that strike your fancy.

Parseltongue Pointers:
- Aln (the River) = "ALAN"
- Alnmouth = "ALAN-muth"
- **Alnwick** (Village and Castle) = "**ANN-ick**"
- Northumberland = "north-UM-ber-lund"

Alnwick Castle dates back to the late 11th century, near the end of the Norman Conquest, when it was a medieval fortress designed to defend the English border by guarding the road that crosses the River Aln. Its earliest parts were erected some time around 1096 by **Yves de Vescy**, **1st** *Baron* **of Alnwick**.

Alnwick Castle was purchased in 1309 by another Baron, **Henry Percy**. As the **1st** *Lord* **of Alnwick**, Henry Percy began the first of many major castle restorations and additions during the hundreds of years the Percy family has lived there.

In fact, because the Percys have lived in Alnwick Castle for over 700 years, Alnwick Castle is officially considered the second largest, continuously-inhabited castle in all of England—**Windsor Castle** being the largest.

To learn more about Alnwick Castle's colorful history, visit the marvelously-condensed Alnwick Castle page of **Time Travel Britain**'s website:
http://www.timetravel-britain.com/articles/castles/alnwick.shtml

Alnwick Castle is Enormous!

[©2007 Gail Johnson, http://www.gailsgallery.co.uk/]

Occupying more than five acres of land (217,800 square feet / 20,234.282 square meters), Alnwick Castle consists of two irregular rings of stone battlements and buildings. The inner ring is a large bailey (courtyard) surrounded by at least ten interconnected buildings, most of which are several stories high. The huge outer ring is populated by the Barbican and Gatehouse, several medieval towers, two large medieval courtyards, and a southern range of interconnected buildings that currently house the **International Study Programme for Saint Cloud State University, Minnesota, USA**.

Alnwick Castle—Site 44

The Alnwick Castle Shop and Café are found in one of the large courtyards. The other courtyard (*just beyond* the lower left corner of the photo above) contains the Knight's Quest and Dragon Quest exhibitions.

The current Duke—**Ralph Richard Percy, 12th Duke of Northumberland**—and his family occupy only a small portion of the castle. Each spring and summer the bulk of Alnwick Castle is open to the public. Tourist income enables the Percys to maintain and preserve all of the castle's contents and architecture, to fund frequent improvements designed to enhance visitors' experience, and ensure future tourist trade.

As of 2012, portions of at least **17 major motion pictures** and **21 televisions shows** have been filmed at Alnwick Castle.

The first movie filmed at Alnwick Castle was *Becket*, in 1964—a Paramount Pictures movie starring Richard Burton, Peter O'Toole, and John Gielgud.
http://www.imdb.com/title/tt0057877/

The first television show filmed here was *Count Dracula*, in 1977.
http://www.imdb.com/title/tt0075882/

Sorcerer's Stone scenes were filmed at Alnwick Castle in October of 2000, followed by *Chamber of Secrets* filming in March of 2002.

Please Note: Although many Internet sources (including Wikipedia) often list Alnwick Castle as being a film site for several other Harry Potter movies—including the two *Deathly Hallows* films—that information is **false**. Only *Sorcerer's Stone* and *Chamber of Secrets* scenes (and background plates) were filmed here.
http://www.alnwickcastle.com/explore/film-and-tv

😀😀😀 If we had a *Triple* Great Site rating, Alnwick Castle would earn it. No other UK film site has so enthusiastically embraced and accommodated Harry Potter fans.

In addition to plenty of Potter-Specific and Potter-Related tours, activities and exhibits, Alnwick Castle offers a multitude of interesting Non-Potter events and performances. Furthermore, enjoyment of all these tours, activities and exhibits, events and performers, are *included* in the Alnwick Castle admission fee.

Daily Alnwick Castle Potter-Specific Offerings

Go to the *What's On* webpage and click on the **Show All** link to discover what is scheduled on the dates you're considering for your visit.
http://www.alnwickcastle.com/whats-on

When you arrive at the Castle, check the **Schedule Board** and note the day's event times.

Broomstick Training Sessions!

"Master your broomstick and take your first flying lesson with our resident wizards ... Broomsticks provided. See times on arrival."

[©2011 Connor Denman]

At least 2 broomstick flying training sessions are offered each day, lasting approximately 15 minutes and followed by 5 minutes of photo-taking time.
http://www.alnwickcastle.com/events/63/broomstick-training

Battleaxes to Broomsticks Tours are offered at least twice daily and last approximately 45 minutes. During the Summer Season, up to four tours are offered each day. A costumed Tour Guide will take you to all of the Harry Potter film sites, as well as to sites where other movies and TV shows have been shot. If you like, you can repeat the tour and enjoy another Guide's perspective—something we highly recommend.

Stationary Guides are posted. If you don't have time to join a tour, not to worry. Each major Alnwick Castle area is overseen by a Stationary Guide who can regale you with information about the Harry Potter filming that took place.

Please Note: If information provided by any Alnwick Guide contradicts *Harry Potter Places* information, **Mum's The Word**. Quietly enjoy the fact that you have a guidebook that has been painstakingly researched, and is more likely to be accurate than the script of the Alnwick Castle Guides.

Costumed Harry Potter Characters perform and pose for pix on two or three weekends (often including Fridays) during each summer month.

Alnwick Castle—Site 44

Somewhat Potter-Related Entertainments

Alnwick Castle's **Knight's Quest Exhibit** and **Dragon Quest Exhibit** are offered daily at intervals, usually between 11am and 4pm.
http://www.alnwickcastle.com/explore/whats-here/knights-quest

Non-Potter Entertainments

The *What's On* Alnwick Castle webpage also provides info about terrific Non-Potter offerings that may be scheduled, including:
- Grounds and History Tour
- Medieval Crafts
- Medieval Jesting
- Raphael Medieval Falconry
- Swordsmanship

And *many* others!

The Alnwick Castle Gift Shop

Of all the UK Potter film sites, Alnwick Castle's Gift Shop has the largest selection of Harry Potter souvenirs. You can buy Harry Potter robes, plastic eyeglasses and wands, a Hagrid mask with attached wig and beard, action figures and pin badges, as well as models of iconic items such as the Sorting Hat, a Golden Snitch, and the Knight Bus.

The Alnwick Castle shop also sells inexpensive, simple wood and broom-straw Halloween broomsticks, similar to those seen in Madame Hooch's *SS Flying Lesson*.

Consider visiting the gift shop and **purchasing props** *before* you tour Alnwick Castle.

Sipping and Supping at Alnwick Castle

Enjoy inexpensive fare purchased from the **Medieval Courtyard food stands**, chow down in the casual **Courtyard Café**, or go whole-Hogwarts and dine in the posh **Hotspur Restaurant**.
http://www.alnwickcastle.com/eat

The Alnwick Castle Potter Places Map

We highly recommend that Potterites plan to enjoy at least *one* Battleaxe to Broomsticks tour—*without* worrying about snapping screenshot reproductions while touring. Our **Alnwick Castle Potter Places Map** is designed to help you visit the **Five Harry Potter film sites** before or after touring—or, instead of touring, if your time here is severely limited.

Harry Potter Places Book Four

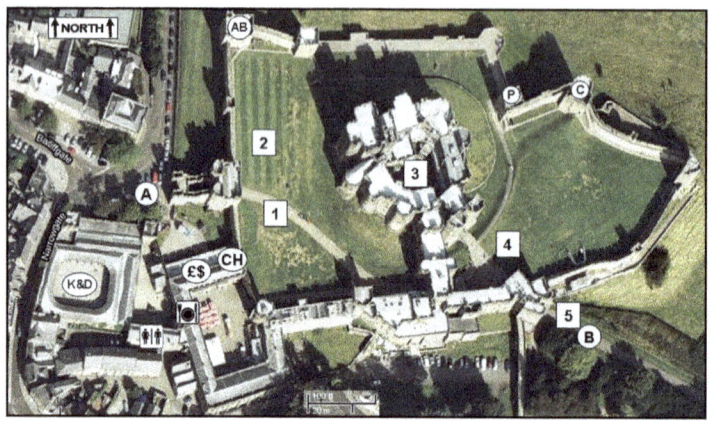

[Underlying map ©2009 Google Maps UK]
http://www.HarryPotterPlaces.com/b4/AlnwickPotterMap.pdf

Also included in the Alnwick Castle Potter Places PDF are four maps related to Alnwick Village **parking options** and **walking directions** for Potterites who park or arrive by Bus.

The Alnwick Castle Potter Places Map Key

Numbers in boxes identify the five Harry Potter film sites.

The Alnwick Castle Potter Pix guide (below) explains what was filmed at each of these locations.

Circled Letters and Symbols identify Alnwick Castle structures.

A Main Castle Entrance, Barbican and Gatehouse, on Bailiffgate (street)

AB Abbot's Tower, Regimental Museum of the Royal Northumberland Fusiliers

B Secondary Castle Entrance (facing Alnwick Garden)
   Please Note: You cannot enter via this gate unless you've already purchased a Castle ticket—either **online** or at **Alnwick Garden**.

C Constable's Tower, Napoleonic wars military displays

CH Coach House

K&D Knight's Quest and Dragon Quest Exhibit areas

P Postern Tower, Dukes of Northumberland exhibit and Antiquities Museum

Alnwick Castle—Site 44

 £$ Shop

 Medieval Courtyard food stands and Café

 Public Toilets

Alnwick Castle Potter Pix

Map Box #1: Broomstick Lessons

The following five *Sorcerer's Stone* **screenshots (enhanced)** are best reproduced during, and at the end of, a Broomstick Flying Lesson—especially since Alnwick Castle provides all Flying Lesson students with brooms!

21

Obviously, you cannot *reproduce* the screenshot above. But, you can photograph the real-life Alnwick Castle torch mounted here.

When recreating this screenshot, be sure to have your Neville stand-in collapsed on the ground immediately beneath the arrow slit just north of the Barbican Gatehouse's door.

Alnwick Castle—Site 44

Map Box #2: Quidditch Lessons

The first of the following two screenshots shows Harry and Oliver Wood exiting the Barbican Gatehouse's door, and could more accurately be considered a Map Box #1 location pic. But, because the bulk of Harry's Quidditch lesson footage was shot in the area just north of Map Box #1, Map Box #2 identifies the Quidditch lessons film site.

[*Sorcerer's Stone* screenshots (enhanced) above and below]

Map Box #3: Hogwarts Courtyard Scenes

[*Sorcerer's Stone* screenshots (enhanced) above and below]

Map Box #4: Another Hogwarts Courtyard and the Flying Ford Anglia Landing Site

[*Sorcerer's Stone* screenshot (enhanced)]

Alnwick Castle—Site 44

[*Chamber of Secrets* screenshot (enhanced)]

Alas, there is no Whomping Willow at Alnwick Castle.

When background plates for *COS* scenes featuring the Whomping Willow were shot at Alnwick Castle, two real-life Ford Anglias were actually present—one of which was *suspended in the air* by a crane.

[*Chamber of Secrets* screenshot segments (enhanced)]

Unfortunately, this beloved tree was entirely created by CGI magic, and doesn't exist.

Map Box #5: Flying Ford Anglia Tunnel and Gate Leading to Hagrid's Hut

The tunnel that connects the area of Map Box #4 with the **Secondary Castle Entrance**—the exit to **Alnwick Garden**—is where the screenshot below was filmed.

Harry Potter Places Book Four

[*Chamber of Secrets* screenshot (enhanced)]

The Gate that led from Hogwarts to Hagrid's Hut in *Sorcerer's Stone* is the **Secondary Castle Entrance**—the exit to **Alnwick Garden**.

[*Sorcerer's Stone* screenshots (enhanced) above and below]

Alnwick Castle—Site 44

A Special Potter Pic Opportunity

Approximately two blocks south of Alnwick Castle's Bailiffgate Main Entrance is a street called **Pottergate**! Little more than a block long, Pottergate runs west from **Narrowgate** road to the **Pottergate Tower**—an 18th century rebuild of a Medieval Gate that was one of four access points back when Alnwick Village was enclosed by a protective stone wall.

You cannot miss Pottergate. A lantern-topped, stone water fountain is mounted in the middle of its eastern mouth at Narrowgate. Walk a few feet west from the fountain on Pottergate and **turn left into the first lane—a lane** *also* **called Pottergate**. Look to your right for the Pottergate sign mounted on a stone wall.

[©2009 Google Maps UK street view segments (enhanced)]

The maps on pages 2, 3, and 5 of our Alnwick Castle Potter Maps PDF show the location of both Pottergate streets, with a **red X** marking the Pottergate sign site.

The **circled-T** on those maps identifies Pottergate Tower. Sadly, the tower doesn't sport a plaque on its side, and you cannot climb to its top. **Thus, there are no Potter Pic opportunities at Pottergate Tower**.

Non-Potter Places at Alnwick Castle

Several exciting exhibitions and museums are housed within three of Alnwick Castle's medieval towers, and within the Coach House next to the Shop and Café. Your admission ticket includes entry to all these features, and all are briefly described within the **Alnwick Castle pamphlet** you'll receive upon arrival.

Harry Potter Places Book Four

Circled Letters on Our Alnwick Castle Potter Places Map:

AB Abbot's Tower contains the Regimental Museum of the Royal Northumberland Fusiliers.
http://www.northumberlandfusiliers.org.uk/

C Constable's Tower houses military displays related to the Napoleonic wars (1798-1814), such as the **Percy Tenantry Volunteers** exhibition.

CH The Coach House contains a small collection of antique transportation devices, ranging from the Northumberland Ducal Coach to sedan chairs and bicycles.

P Postern Tower contains an historical exhibit about the Dukes of Northumberland and their interest in **archaeology**. It also houses an **Antiquities Museum** with displays including mosaics from Pompeii, relics from Ancient Egypt, and Romano-British objects.

Alnwick Garden
http://www.alnwickgarden.com/
http://en.wikipedia.org/wiki/The_Alnwick_Garden

Just southeast of Alnwick Castle is the spectacularly gorgeous **Alnwick Garden**. We strongly encourage garden-loving Potterites to schedule an entire day in Alnwick so you can visit *both* the Castle and Garden.

Opening Times: Alnwick Garden is open daily from 10am to 6pm during the season (between March 31st and November 5th, 2012).

Alnwick Garden Only Ticket: Adults £12.00 ($19), Seniors £10.80 ($17), Children 5-16 years old £4 ($6), under-5 years old free.

Combined Alnwick Garden and Alnwick Castle Ticket: Adults £24.00 ($39), Seniors £21.60 ($35), Children 5-16 years old £10.00 ($16), under-5 years old free.

Alnwick Castle Only Tickets are also sold at Alnwick Garden's Main Entrance, in case you park in the Alnwick Garden car park (see page 4 of the Alnwick Castle Potter Maps PDF) and want to enter Alnwick Castle via the Secondary Entrance.

Alnwick Castle—Site 44

Discounted Family tickets (2 adults with up to 4 children) for the Garden or Castle are available online or onsite.

Online Discount: If purchased online, you'll receive a **5% discount** on *any* form of Alnwick ticket.

The original **Alnwick Garden** dates back to 1750, when Hugh Percy, the 1st Duke of Northumberland, hired **Capability Brown** to design and supervise construction of his estate's ornamental garden. Subsequent Percy generations improved and expanded it until **WWII**, when all 12 acres (at that time) were plowed under so that **food** could be produced during the *Dig For Victory* campaign.
http://www.homesweethomefront.co.uk/web_pages/hshf_dig_for_victory_pg.htm

Sadly, Alnwick Garden was entirely abandoned after the war, and gradually disappeared beneath decades of overgrowth.

In 1997, **Jane Percy**—the current and **12th Duchess of Northumberland**—stumbled upon the old Alnwick garden. Although little more than brambles and broken brickwork remained, Her Grace was instantly inspired by the natural magic of the site, and dreamed of restoring it so as to create a **gigantic public garden**.

Soon thereafter, Jane Percy's husband admirably donated **42 acres** to the **Alnwick Garden Trust** charity, with the Duchess serving as trustee and volunteering her time to drive the Alnwick Garden project forward.
http://www.alnwickgarden.com/get-involved/charitable-projects

Phase one of the modern day Alnwick Garden opened in October of 2001, after completion of **The Grand Cascade** with its fabulous array of fountains and waterfalls. Many additional features have opened since then, such as the **Ornamental Garden**, **Rose Garden**, **Bamboo Labyrinth**, and **Cherry Orchard**. Situated in a **Lime Tree Grove**, the **Alnwick Garden Tree House** complex opened in 2004, and is one of the largest tree houses in the world.

Several additional features are currently under development. With 42 acres to fill, Alnwick Garden is likely to grow larger and larger with every passing year.

Special Potter Note: Mandrake plants can be found in the **Poison Garden** that was opened in 2005. Surrounded by a strong fence and kept securely locked at all times, **Guards** are posted at this garden's gate to prevent uncontrolled access to the dangerous plants contained within. Approximately every 20 minutes throughout the day, the Guards become **Guides**, and escort groups of visitors on a tour of the Poison Garden—more often if a large crowd has gathered.

Harry Potter Places Book Four

Alnwick Lodging Options

If you'll only be stopping at Alnwick Castle for a few hours while traveling between **Goathland (Site #46)** and **Edinburgh (Part One of *Harry Potter Places* Book Five—Scotland: Hogwarts' Home)**, explore lodgings in the location you'll reach at the end of your Alnwick Castle visit day.

Potterites who can spend a full day enjoying Alnwick Castle (and Garden) will find a surprisingly wide variety of lodging options located within the center of Alnwick Village.

Check in Cheap: The Alnwick Youth Hostel
http://www.yha.org.uk/hostel/alnwick

Google Maps UK: 34 – 38 Green Batt, Alnwick, Northumberland NE66 1TU

SatNav/GPS for Roxboro Place Pay & Display car park: 55.412067,-1.705275

[See **P**4 on page 3 of the Alnwick Castle Potter Maps PDF]
  Part of the **England & Wales Youth Hostels Association** (YHA), the **Alnwick Youth Hostel** is available to Potterites of all ages, and is only a 9 minute walk from Alnwick Castle's Bailiffgate Main Entrance, or an 8 minute walk from Alnwick Garden. The hostel is located on Green Batt Street, approximately 5 blocks south and east from the Alnwick Bus Station. Onsite parking is available only for *pre-booked* **disabled access**, but the Roxboro Place Pay & Display car park is just around the corner. **WiFi** and **Laundry facilities** are available here, as is a restaurant and self-catering kitchen.

Board at the Burrow: Alnwick Bed & Breakfast Establishments

The Leaky Cauldron to Malfoy Manor: Livable to Luxurious Alnwick Hotels

Explore the **Visit Alnwick** website's accommodation links to learn about the many Alnwick B&B and Hotel options:
http://www.visitalnwick.org.uk/accommodation.htm

Going to Alnwick Castle
Public Transportation
http://www.nationalrail.co.uk/

Approximately 4 miles from the village of Alnwick, the nearest Railway Station is in the village of **Alnmouth**. Alnmouth Railway Station [**ALM**]

Alnwick Castle—Site 44

is a regular stop on the East Coast service between London Kings Cross and Edinburgh.

Please Note: There is no Luggage Storage or Taxi Rank at ALM, nor at the Alnmouth or Alnwick Bus Stations.

🚌 **Busses to the Alnwick Bus Station** (which is little more than a bus parking lot) are readily available at the Alnmouth Bus Station, a 2 minute walk from ALM. The bus journey between Alnmouth and Alnwick is only about 15 minutes. Be sure to ask the driver for a return bus schedule.

Alnwick Castle and Garden is only an 8 minute walk from the Alnwick Bus Station [see page 5 of our Alnwick Castle Potter Maps PDF].

🚕 **To take a Taxi from ALM to Alnwick Castle or Garden**, you'll need to contact a local service and *prebook* **a cab** to meet you at the Alnmouth Railway Station.

The following Alnwick Taxi services have websites.
http://cheaptaxialnwick.co.uk/
http://www.knightstaxi.com/
http://alnwick.inuklocal.co.uk/Transport/Taxis/Petes-Taxis-117-10533
http://www.taxialnmouth.com/
http://www.theyellowtaxi.co.uk/

Be sure to also prebook your return trip. Beware of Taxi drivers who insist they can quickly come and get you when you call them. The wait for *any* Taxi called from Alnwick Castle or Garden—even using the driver's personal phone number—can sometimes be **well over an hour**.

If you aren't sure how long you'll be spending in Alnwick, prebook a Taxi to take you *to* the Castle or Garden, then walk to Alnwick Bus Station after your visit and catch the next bus back to ALM. You can snag your Pottergate pic on the way to the bus station.

Alnwick Castle Public Transportation Luggage Laments

If you're traveling to Alnwick by Rail or Bus and *not* lodging in the village, be prepared to lug your luggage around all day long!

Harry Potter Places Book Four

[©2009 Tara Bellers]

As of 2012, no public luggage storage facility is available within Alnwick Village, at the Castle, or at the Garden. With luck, the letters we've written to Alnwick Castle and Garden will encourage them to eventually install luggage lockers.

You can help! When visiting the Alnwick Castle and Garden websites during your holiday planning, contact them and ask about luggage storage locker availability.
info@alnwickcastle.com
info@alnwickgarden.com

If Alnwick Castle and Garden still don't offer luggage lockers at the time of your contact, you'll at least have **registered a need for this service**, and helped to encourage them to provide it.

In the mean time, the **Alnwick Youth Hostel** has generously offered to assist baggage-burdened Potterites. See the **Check in Cheap** info above and contact them about the possibility of stowing your bags for the day. Unfortunately, if the Alnwick YHA is heavily booked on your visit date, they'll not have room to store your luggage.

Driving to Alnwick Castle

The best SatNav/GPS coordinates for reaching Alnwick are those that lead to **parking places**, and **the length of your intended stay** dictates the parking places best for your needs.

Please Note: If you're planning to only spend 2 to 4 hours at Alnwick Castle, but your itinerary is *flexible* and allows for a potentially longer visit, **park in a Long Stay lot** and **pay for more than 4 hours**. That way, you'll avoid having to move your car after discovering that we weren't exaggerating about how much fun you'll have at Alnwick Castle.

Alnwick Castle—Site 44

Alnwick Village Parking for Less Than 4 Hours

[Page 2 of the Alnwick Castle Potter Maps PDF]

P1: Bailiffgate Street offers parking spaces closest to Alnwick Castle's Main Entrance. Obviously, these street spaces fill up quite quickly. But, considering the convenience of parking so near, it is certainly worth seeing if a space is open before heading to a more distant car park—especially if you'll be arriving early in the morning.

🚗 **Bailiffgate Street SatNav/GPS:** 14 Bailiffgate, Alnwick, Northumberland NE66 1, UK

[©2008 C.D. Miller]

You can park on Bailiffgate Street, free of charge, for up to 4 hours.

To extend your stay, you may be able to avoid the **No-return-fine** by moving your car to a different space—preferably on the *other* side of the street—just before your first 4 hours are up.

P2: The Pottergate Pay & Display Lot. Maximum stay between 8am and 6pm is 4 hours, and costs £1.50 ($2). To extend your stay without being fined, you must move to a different car park—or to a space on Bailiffgate Street.

🚗 There are three SatNav/GPS options for finding the Pottergate car park:
- Pottergate, Alnwick, Northumberland NE66 1JT
- 55.414187,-1.710092
- NE66 1JT

Alnwick Village Parking for More Than 4 Hours
[Page 3 of the Alnwick Castle Potter Maps PDF]
   Please Note: If you're planning to only spend 2 to 4 hours at Alnwick Castle, but end up parking in a Long-Stay lot because the Short-Term lots are full, go ahead and pay for **over 4 hours**—it's not that much more expensive.

Harry Potter Places Book Four

🅿 **3: Dispensary Street Pay & Display Car Park.**

🚗 **SatNav/GPS:** 55.413182,-1.710098

Alternative **SatNav/GPS:** Fenkle Street, Alnwick, NE66 1HE

The Fenkle Street coordinates above are for the front entrance of **Morrisons Supermarket**. Morrisons' parking lot is *behind* the supermarket, on Lagny Street. The Dispensary Street car park is across the street from Morrisons' parking lot. If you use the Fenkle Street coordinates, watch for signs directing you to Morrisons' car park—you may be able to drive down an alley to reach it *from* Fenkle Street.

Alternatively, from the south end of Fenkle Street, drive west on Clayport Street and turn right to drive north on Lagny Street. When you see the Morrisons' parking lot on your right, look left for the Dispensary Street Pay & Display car park.

Parking Tariffs between 8am and 6pm: £1 ($2) for 2 hours, £1.50 ($2)for 4 hours, £2 ($3) for over 4 hours.

🅿 **4: Roxboro Place Pay & Display Car Park.**

🚗 **SatNav/GPS:** 55.412067,-1.705275

Alternative **SatNav/GPS:** 34 – 38 Green Batt, Alnwick, Northumberland NE66 1TU

The Green Batt coordinates above are for the **Alnwick Youth Hostel**. The entrance to Roxboro Place Pay & Display car park is just east of there, on the north side of Green Batt Street.

Parking Tariffs between 8am and 6pm: £1 ($2) for 2 hours, £1.50 ($2)for 4 hours, £2 ($3) for over 4 hours.

🅿 **5: Greenwell Road Long-Stay Pay & Display Car Parks.**

🚗 **SatNav/GPS:** Town Centre, Greenwell Road, Alnwick NE66 1HB, *or* 55.413876,-1.705168

You'll pass the Greenwell Road *Short-Stay* Pay & Display car parks (2-hour max) while driving north on Greenwell Road, then round a bend and head northwest to the Long-Stay lots.

Parking Tariffs between 8am and 6pm: £1.50 ($2)for 4 hours, £2 ($3) for over 4 hours.

The Alnwick Garden Car Park

[Page 4 of the Alnwick Castle Potter Maps PDF]

🚗 **SatNav/GPS:** 55.415219,-1.694743, *or* Denwick Ln, Alnwick, Northumberland NE66 9

Only a 3 to 5 minute walk east of Alnwick Garden—a 10 to 15 minute walk from Alnwick Castle's Secondary (back) Entrance—this car park is the

Alnwick Castle—Site 44

farthest from Alnwick Castle's Main Entrance, at least a 25 minute walk. The Garden car park lot fee is also the most expensive in Alnwick: £3 ($5), no matter how long or short your stay.

However, because the Alnwick Garden car park is so large, you're absolutely assured of finding a parking place here. And, this parking place is good for the full length of your visit—no matter how long you might stay.

Harry Potter Places Book Four

45

Durham Cathedral

Hogwarts Castle and Professor McGonagall's Classroom
http://www.durhamcathedral.co.uk/
http://en.wikipedia.org/wiki/Durham_Cathedral
http://www.durhamworldheritagesite.com/architecture/cathedral

Google Maps UK: Durham Cathedral, Durham DH1 3EH *or* 54.773611, -1.576111

🚗 **SatNav/GPS coordinates** and parking tips are provided in the **Driving to Durham Cathedral** section.

Operation Hours and Entry Fees information is provided below.

Visit Time: Schedule *at least* 2 hours for your visit — 3 to 4 hours if you enjoy historic architecture.

Parseltongue Pointers:
- Durham = "DUR-um"
- Saint Cuthbert = "KUTH-bert" (*not* "KOOTH-bert")

⊰⊱

Officially titled **The Cathedral Church of Christ, Blessed Mary the Virgin, and St Cuthbert of Durham**, this magnificent example of Norman architecture is commonly known as **Durham Cathedral**. Construction of its earliest portions began in 1093 and took 40 years to complete. Originally a **Benedictine Monastery**, it became one of the most important **Church of England** Cathedrals in 1539 — after Henry VIII disbanded and either destroyed or repurposed all Catholic monasteries, priories, convents and friaries in England, Wales and Ireland.

During the 17th and 18th centuries, Durham Cathedral suffered numerous indignities, including some grievous alterations of its original Norman structure. Thankfully, much of what had been damaged was restored during

Harry Potter Places Book Four

the 19th century. And, in 1986, Durham Cathedral was designated a United Nations Educational, Scientific and Cultural Organization (UNESCO) **World Heritage Site**, thus ensuring its ongoing protection and preservation.

Durham Cathedral's relationship with Harry Potter began in October of 2000, when *Sorcerer's Stone* scenes were filmed there, followed by the shooting of *Chamber of Secrets* scenes in March of 2002. Although no other location filming took place there after that, exterior and interior aspects of Durham Cathedral have been reflected throughout **all** the Harry Potter movies: in the design of Hogwarts Castle's CGI exterior, Hogwarts background plates, and Hogwarts interior sets.

No photography is allowed within Durham Cathedral proper.

Happily, the Cathedral area is *not* a Potter film site. All Potter scenes were shot within Durham's four **Cloister Ranges**, the **Cloister Garth**, the **Chapter House**, and from the top of the Cathedral's **Central Tower**. And, all of these areas are publicly accessible, *except for* the Chapter House (more info about that in the Potter Pix directions).

The Durham Cathedral Potter Map

To help Potterites find each of the film sites, we created the **Durham Cathedral Potter Map**, and posted it on the *Harry Potter Places* website.
http://www.HarryPotterPlaces.com/b4/DurhamPotterMap.pdf

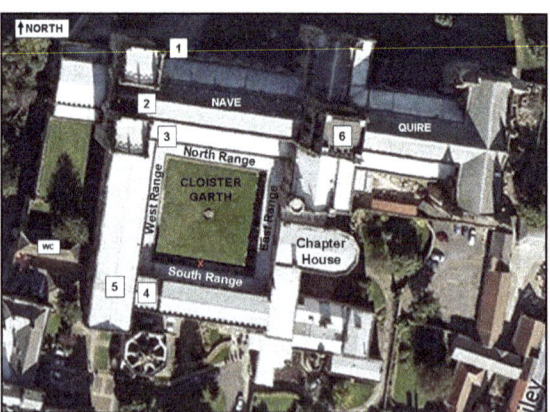

[Underlying image (enhanced and edited) ©2011 Google Maps UK]

Durham Cathedral—Site 45

The Durham Cathedral Potter Map KEY

1 Durham Cathedral's **Main Entrance**, once known as the **North Portal**.

2 Information Desk

3 Durham Cloisters Entrance

4 The **Monastic Great Kitchen** that houses the **Cathedral Gift Shop**. (During 2012 renovations, the shop is being moved to the Undercroft.)

5 Undercroft Restaurant

6 Central Tower

WC The **Water Closet** (public toilet) is accessed *through* the restaurant.

X marks the spot of the **Cloister Garth Access Gate**.

Operation Hours, Entry Fees, and Special Tours

Durham Cathedral is open for worship and private prayer from 7:30am to 6pm on Mondays through Saturdays, and from 7:45am to 5:30pm on Sundays.

Durham Cathedral Cloisters are open from 9am to 6pm on Mondays through Saturdays, and from 10am to 6pm on Sundays.

During Summer Months, the Cathedral and Cloisters are open until 8pm every day.

There is no Entry Fee for Durham Cathedral or the Cloisters.

> "However, it costs more than £60,000 a week to maintain the Cathedral [and Cloisters] ... for which we receive no state aid. Therefore, we ask visitors to make a generous donation."

Polite Potterites should generously donate to Durham Cathedral.

Potter to the Top of the Central Tower

The tallest of Durham Cathedral's three towers, the Central Tower is 218 feet (66 m) high. The top can be accessed by robust Potterites able to climb up a tight-spiral stone staircase, consisting of **325** very shallow, narrow, and steep steps. To preview a snippet of this staircase, go to **A Climb to the top of the Tower of Durham Cathedral—Part 1:**
http://www.youtube.com/watch?v=2a7--UzSv-I&feature=related

Because the Tower climb is so strenuous and potentially precarious, Cathedral Stewards deny access to those who fail to meet very strict rules.
- Suitable footwear must be worn. Open-toed shoes or sandals, or any shoes with high heels, are prohibited. Trainers (tennis shoes) and any other form of closed-toe, flat-soled shoes are fine.

- All children must be accompanied by an adult, with no more than two children per adult.

- Children must be able to climb the steps independently—they cannot be carried.

- Climbers must have both hands free. All rucksacks and bags must be left with the Cathedral Stewards at the bottom of the Tower. If your camera cannot be hung around your neck, stuff it in a pocket before being checked by the Stewards.

The Tower is open year round (weather permitting), but is closed during Services and special events. To check the times of availability on the day you plan to visit, contact the Chapter Office: enquiries@durhamcathedral.co.uk

Common Opening Times:
Monday to Saturday (April—September), 10am to 4pm.
Monday to Saturday (October—March), 10am to 3pm.
Sundays, 1pm to 2:30pm.

Admission Fee: Adults £5 ($8), accompanied children under 16 years old £2.50 ($4). No discounted *Concessions* (Senior or Student) tickets are offered.

Cathedral Tours for Individual Visitors

Guided Cathedral Tours are available between April and October on Mondays through Saturdays, usually at 10:30am, 11am and 2pm. No reservation is required, but times and the number of tours may vary, depending on the number of volunteer guides available on any given day. Tours are not offered on Sundays, or during special Services and events. To check availability and times of a Cathedral Tour on the day of your visit, contact the Chapter Office: enquiries@durhamcathedral.co.uk

Tour Fee: Adults £5 ($8), Seniors and Students £4.50 ($7), accompanied children under 16 years old are admitted free.
  Please Note: While these tours are not Potter-centric and will not gain you access to the Chapter House, they are well worth taking. Durham Cathedral Guides provide interesting historical commentary about each of the public areas they lead you to, such as:

Durham Cathedral—Site 45

- The Cathedral Nave and Quire
- The Shrine of St Cuthbert
- The Galilee Chapel
- The Cloisters

See the **Durham World Heritage website** to learn about the public areas listed above, as well as other areas of interest contained within Durham Cathedral, such as:
- The Monks' Dormitory
- The Monastic Great Kitchen. (When renovations begun in 2012 are completed, the **Treasures of Saint Cuthbert**—a fabulous exhibit currently confined to storage—will be displayed here.)
- The Chapel of the Nine Altars
- The Durham Cathedral Organs

http://www.durhamworldheritagesite.com/architecture/cathedral/intro

Information about the Undercroft Restaurant and Cathedral Shop can be found on Durham Cathedral's *What to Visit* webpage:
http://www.durhamcathedral.co.uk/visiting/attractions

An Early December Visit may be Potterly Problematic

Each year, during the first weekend of December, the city of Durham holds a spectacular **Victorian Christmas Festival**.
http://www.durhamchristmasfestival.com/

> "...cobbled streets [filled] with entertainers, reindeer for the children ... over 150 quality craft, gift and food stalls in a huge marquee on Palace Green. ... falconry displays, free pony and trap rides, tile painting workshops, a juggler, a live nativity scene and more."

Durham Cathedral's Christmas Festival participation includes providing carolers and **hosting a local producers' market** *within the Cloisters*. During the festival, produce vendor booths line the Cloister Ranges. With far greater-than-normal numbers of Muggles milling about during this event, Potter screenshot reproduction becomes practically impossible. To preview the Christmas Festival Cloisters Market, go to:
http://www.youtube.com/watch?v=AMdIAMsxqrk

Many Potterites will thoroughly enjoy visiting during Durham's Victorian Christmas Festival! If you're not one of those Potterites, avoid Durham Cathedral during the first weekend of December.

Durham Cathedral Potter Pix

Refer to the **Durham Cathedral Potter Map** to follow our directions.

Harry Potter Places Book Four

Enter Durham Cathedral via the main entrance (**North Portal**), and go to the **Information Desk**. Check the times of Central Tower access and/or Individual Cathedral Tours, then plan your visit accordingly. When ready to take your Cloister area Potter Pix, head for the **Cloister Entrance**.

Walk forward into the **West Cloister Range**. The first two Potter Pix are Cloister Garth scenes shot *from* the West Range. Unfortunately, the stone benches were set pieces, and don't exist in real-life.

If you have companions who can pose as Potter people stand-ins, find a Cathedral Steward and politely ask that the **Cloister Garth Access Gate** in the South Range be unlocked so that you can send them into the Garth.

Additionally (or alternatively), send your companions ahead to perch in the arches of the East Cloister Range while you take pix from the West Range.

Durham Cathedral Potter Pix #1 and #2

[*Chamber of Secrets* screenshots (enhanced) above and below]

Durham Cathedral—Site 45

When you reach the end of the West Range, turn left and walk about ten feet down the **South Cloister Range**, then perform an about-face. The portal seen in the background of the screenshot below is the door that leads to the **Undercroft Restaurant**.

Durham Cathedral Potter Pic #3

[*Chamber of Secrets* screenshot (enhanced)]

While still in the South Range, turn your attention to the middle of Durham Cathedral's **Cloister Garth**. There you'll see an ancient stone basin that served as a **lavatory** (washing place) for the Benedictine Monks who lived here in the 11th century.

[©2009 Tara Bellers]

Harry Potter Places Book Four

For Harry Potter filming, this basin was enhanced with a fountain-like pedestal set piece. The next three screenshots are Cloister Garth scenes shot *from* the South Cloister Range. Again, if you have Potter stand-ins available, ask a Cathedral Steward to unlock the South Range Garth gate.

Durham Cathedral Potter Pix #4 and #5

[*Sorcerer's Stone* screenshots (enhanced) above and below]

Durham Cathedral Potter Pic #6

After launching from Harry's arm, Hedwig flew past Durham Cathedral's Central Tower. This angle of the Central Tower can be shot from Durham's South Cloister Range.

Durham Cathedral—Site 45

[*Sorcerer's Stone* screenshot (enhanced)]

The Chapter House
http://www.durhamworldheritagesite.com/architecture/cathedral/intro/chapter-house

Turn left at the end of the South Range. About half-way down the **East Cloister Range** you'll find the door to the **Chapter House** where **Professor McGonagall's classroom scenes** were filmed for *SS* and *COS*. Three sides of this room's marvelous Norman architecture sport an unmistakable march of stone-carved column façades, topped by intersecting arches.

[*Chamber of Secrets* screenshot (enhanced)]

Since the release of *Sorcerer's Stone* in 2001, visiting Potterites have often pleaded for public access to the Chapter House. Unfortunately, Durham Cathedral continues to deny it—for several reasons.

Cathedral officials prefer to downplay the Cathedral's role as a frequent film site for major motion pictures and television shows.

> "Groups or individuals seeking information concerning the filming [of *SS* or *COS*] will find that Cathedral stewards and guides are more than willing to talk about the history and architecture of this 900 year old place of worship rather than the short time when it was used as a location for these two films."

However, the possibility of opening the Chapter House to the public *was* investigated in 2006—after all, it is a significant section of the 11th century Benedictine Monastery's claustral buildings. Among other findings, the investigation determined that:

• The Chapter House is a secure working space, used every day by Cathedral Vergers, clergy and choir.

• Two other rooms vital to facilitating Cathedral services and operation can only be accessed from the Chapter House.

• There is no alternative space for the essential uses of the Chapter House.

The 2006 Conclusion: Opening the Chapter House to the public would seriously interfere with the worship life of Durham Cathedral.

Although polite Potterites will agree that interference with Durham Cathedral's worship life is a bad thing, all is not lost! The locked East Cloister Range Chapter House door is flanked by two leaded glass windows.

[©2009 Tara Bellers]

With *!!!Flash OFF!!!*, hold your camera against the glass of a window *south* of the door (the windows on your *right* when facing the door). By doing this, you can snap a reasonably good Potter Pic of the Chapter House interior—as

Durham Cathedral—Site 45

Wolfgang Mletzko did in 2003 (below). It may take a few snaps to get a pic as wonderful as Wolfgang's. Thank goodness for Digital Cameras!

Durham Cathedral Potter Pic #7

[©2003 Wolfgang Mletzko]

We specify snapping your pix at the glass of a southern window because the southwestern corner of the Chapter House contains an historic **wooden cupboard** that could not be removed for filming. Thus, this cupboard can be spied in both the *SS* and *COS* McGonagall classroom sets.

[*Sorcerer's Stone* screenshot (enhanced)]

Harry Potter Places Book Four

[*Chamber of Secrets* screenshot (enhanced)]

After snapping your Chapter House window pix, remain at the East Range mid-point, but turn to face north (the Chapter House door on your right) to shoot Potter Pix #8 and #9. Move closer to the northern end for Potter Pic #10.

Durham Cathedral Potter Pix #8 and #9

[*Sorcerer's Stone* screenshots (enhanced) above and below]

Durham Cathedral—Site 45

Durham Cathedral Potter Pic #10

[*Chamber of Secrets* screenshot (enhanced)]

When you reach the corner seen above, turn left into the **North Cloister Range**. Here is where scenes of Harry tricking *Lucius Malfoy* into freeing Dobby were filmed. The Garth-side of the South Range is seen in the background of the last two Cloister Potter Pix.

Durham Cathedral Potter Pix #11 and #12

[*Chamber of Secrets* screenshots (enhanced) above and below]

Harry Potter Places Book Four

Alas, the scenes of Dobby discovering the gift sock, and subsequently stupefying his evil former master, significantly relied on CGI magic. None of Durham Cathedral's Cloister Ranges are *flanked* by arched openings, nor is there a door leading outside at the end of the North Range.

[*Chamber of Secrets* screenshot (enhanced)]

Durham Cathedral Central Tower Potter Pix

Robust Potterites who tackle the 325, tightly-spiral, shallow and narrow, stone steps leading to the **Central Tower**'s top will be rewarded with a magnificent aerial view of the City of Durham, the River Wear, County Durham, and beyond. You'll also be able to snap aerial shots of the Cloister Garth that look almost exactly like Pic #13, and relatively similar to the very sad Pic #14. Please ensure that your camera is securely tethered to your wrist before snapping your pix!

Durham Cathedral Potter Pic #13

[*Chamber of Secrets* screenshot (enhanced)]

Durham Cathedral—Site 45

Durham Cathedral Potter Pic #14

[*Half-Blood Prince* screenshot (enhanced)]

A Nearby Non-Potter Place
Durham Castle
http://www.durhamworldheritagesite.com/architecture/castle
http://en.wikipedia.org/wiki/Durham_Castle
http://www.dur.ac.uk/university.college/

Found north of the front of Durham Cathedral, **Durham Castle** is perched upon the same promontory high above the city of Durham. Construction of Durham Castle began in 1072, soon after the Norman Conquest, and few buildings in England can boast a longer history of continuous occupation. During the 900 years following its original completion, the castle's structure has been augmented, extended and altered, in order to meet the challenges of changing circumstances related to its use. Since 1840, Durham Castle has been exclusively occupied by Durham's **University College**.

In 1986, Durham Castle and Durham Cathedral were simultaneously designated as UNESCO **World Heritage Sites**, thus ensuring the castle's ongoing protection and preservation. Durham Castle has additionally become a registered museum.

Because it still functions as a working University and is home to over 100 students, Durham Castle is open to the general public only through guided tours. And, due to last-minute scheduling of University or commercial activities, tours are sometimes canceled with short notice.

If you're a **Castle-Bagger** (someone who seeks to visit as many castles as possible) as well as a Potterite, consult the Durham University webpage related to Durham Castle tours when planning your Durham Cathedral visit.
http://www.dur.ac.uk/university.college.commercial/

🛏 Lodging Options

Durham Cathedral is a between-site foray. Located north of **Goathland** (Site #46), and south of **Alnwick Castle** (Site #44), explore lodgings at the site you'll reach at the end of your Durham visit day.

Going to Durham Cathedral
Public Transportation

Use the directions and links found on the **Directions-to-Durham** page of the *This is Durham* official tourism website.
http://www.thisisdurham.com/site/tourist-information-and-maps/directions-to-durham

🚆 Durham Railway Station [DHM] is approximately a 3-hour train journey from Central London.

🚌 After arriving at DHM, ask for directions to the place where you can board a Bus that will take you to Durham Cathedral. Ask the driver for return bus times and boarding place information before you disembark.

Please Note: Luggage Storage lockers are not available at DHM, within the city, at Durham Cathedral, or at Durham Castle. However, if you'll be Pottering to the top of the Central Tower, do that first. After paying the £5 entry fee, the Stewards will stash your luggage during your climb. Upon your descent, politely ask them to keep it stashed while you Potter in the Cloisters. We suspect that they'll agree, unless Central Tower traffic is particularly heavy on the day of your visit.

Driving to Durham Cathedral
🚗 **SatNav/GPS Driving coordinates:** DH1 3UJ

The post code above is for the **Prince Bishops Shopping Centre** in Durham.
http://www.princebishops.co.uk/

    The Prince Bishops Shopping Centre's multi-level, covered **Car Park** is open 24 hours a day, all year long, and is the most convenient place to park when visiting Durham Cathedral. Prince Bishops' car park entrance is off of west-bound Leazes Road (the A690), at the northeastern area of the Shopping Centre complex. Watch for it on your left when arriving from the east.

    If arriving from the *west*, there is a roundabout just east of the complex. Drive past the complex and follow the roundabout until you are heading back the way you came, and look to your left for the exit lane leading to Prince Bishops Car Park.

Durham Cathedral—Site 45

[Google Maps UK *Street View* screenshot segment (enhanced)]

Drive *past* the Service Vehicle entrance and turn left at the Car Park entrance beneath the **Prince Bishops Durham City Shopping** marquee. There, you'll be issued a plastic **Entry Chip Coin**. Do not loose it! The Lost Chip Coin fee is £15 ($24).

The 2012 parking tariff for 2 to 4 hours is £3.30 ($5), which is sufficient for basic Durham Cathedral Pottering. If you fall under the Cathedral's spell, or also visit Durham Castle, the parking tariff for 4 to 6 hours is £6.20 ($10).

After parking, go up to the **Market Place** street level—the top floor. Head for the Market Place exit to **Silver Street**, and **scan for the nearest Bus Stop**.

🚌 The **Durham Market Place SW-bound** bus will take you to the green between Durham Cathedral and Durham Castle.

Please Note: Google Maps UK correctly identifies the walk from Prince Bishops' Market Place to the green in front of Durham Cathedral as being merely a 0.3 mile/7 minute trek. However, this seemingly-innocent walk is *all uphill*, along a very steep and arduous incline. We strongly recommend **taking a bus *to* Durham Cathedral**, then walking back to the car park after your visit. Your enjoyment of the many colorful and interesting shops along the way will be greatly enhanced while walking *downhill*.

Back at the Shopping Centre, you'll find the payment machine in the lift (elevator) vestibule for your parking level. Insert your Entry Coin Chip and pay to receive an **Exit Coin Chip**. Do not tarry too long at your car before leaving. If you go over the time that you paid for, you'll have to pay extra at the exit.

Harry Potter Places Book Four

46

Goathland Railway Station, Yorkshire

Hogsmead Station, *Sorcerer's Stone*
http://en.wikipedia.org/wiki/Goathland
http://en.wikipedia.org/wiki/Goathland_railway_station
http://www.wonderfulwhitby.co.uk/goathland.html

Google Maps UK and SatNav/GPS: Goathland, North Yorkshire, YO22 5NF

Visit Dates: Avoid driving to Goathland between December and February when snow may obstruct the single-lane roads leading to the village.

Operation Hours: Opening times for Goathland Station facilities are provided below. Goathland shops generally operate from 9am to 5pm in Summer, opening later and closing earlier in Winter.

Visit Time: If you'll not be staying overnight—something we *highly* recommend—schedule at least two hours here.

Parseltongue Pointers:
- Aidensfield = "AID-ens-field" (*not* "IDE-ens-field")
- Goathland = "GOATH-land" (*not* "GOAT-land" or "GOTH-land")
- Yorkshire = "YORK-sher"

☙❧

Goathland is a gorgeous little village nestled high on the **North Yorkshire Moors**, which boasts only 450 residents. The village dates back to Viking times and remained quietly isolated for hundreds of years—until the Railway arrived in 1836. Thereafter, because it was located near several **waterfalls**, Goathland became known as a **spa town**.

This prompted a modest tourist trade and spawned the development of three local hotels, as well as a gaggle of guest houses—something surprising

Harry Potter Places Book Four

for such a small village. Still, Goathland remained relatively unknown until a seemingly insignificant act dramatically changed *everything*.

In 1991, Goathlanders allowed television crews to film a new British police drama within their tiny village. **Heartbeat** was set in the 1960s, and many village buildings were used to depict the show's fictional town of **Aidensfield**. When the first episodes aired in April of 1992, the show became a huge hit. *Heartbeat* continued to film in Goathland during the remarkable **18 seasons** that it was broadcast.
http://en.wikipedia.org/wiki/Heartbeat_%28UK_TV_series%29

Due to the program's popularity, Goathland has become a place of pilgrimage for *Heartbeat* fans, and several village shops have permanently installed the Aidensfield façades associated with the show. *Heartbeat*'s final episodes aired in 2010, but reruns are still seen all over the world. Thus, Aidensfield lives on in Goathland—and always will.

Heartbeat's Special Present for Potterites

[*Chamber of Secrets* screenshots (enhanced)]

At the beginning of *Chamber of Secrets*, the Weasley **Flying Ford Anglia** was used to break Harry out of his Privet Drive bedroom. Later, when prevented from entering Platform 9¾, Ron and Harry used the flying car to reach Hogwarts. Near the end of *COS*, the Flying Ford Anglia roared to the rescue when the boys were trapped in Aragog's Forbidden Forest lair.

By sheer coincidence, the Police vehicle driven by *Heartbeat*'s Bobbies was a **light blue Ford Anglia 105E Deluxe**—exactly the same make and model as the Muggle car modified by Mr. Weasley! Because the Aidensfield Police car is so iconic, there always is at least one of them on display in Goathland. Thus, thanks to *Heartbeat*, this equally-iconic Harry Potter vehicle is available for Potter Pix.

Goathland—Site 46

[©2008 C.D. Miller]

An Aidensfield Police car can usually be found parked in front of the Village Green shops. If one isn't there, continue a block further east (enroute to the Railway Station) to reach the **Goathland Garage and Antique Shop**—aka, **Aidensfield Garage and Scripps Funeral Services**. You're sure to find at least one light blue Ford Anglia 105E Deluxe there.

[©2008 C.D. Miller]

Happy Development: Now that Goathland has also become a Potterite place of pilgrimage, the vehicle most often parked in front of village Post Office is an *unmarked*, light blue Ford Anglia 105E Deluxe. This car looks even more like Mr. Weasley's Flying Ford Anglia than the Aidensfield police cars.

[©2009 Tara Bellers]

Goathland Sheep

Goathland is surrounded by miles and miles of open moorland, most of which is owned by the **Duchy of Lancaster**. Hundreds of years ago, the Duchy's black-faced **Swaledale sheep** were granted a common right to freely graze throughout the moorland, as well as within the village. Because this grant remains in effect, sheep are encountered *everywhere* when visiting Goathland.

[©2008 C.D. Miller]

Sheep Shoulds and Shouldn'ts
• **Sheep *always* have the Right of Way**. If you encounter one or more of them while driving on the single-lane road leading to Goathland, stop and wait for the sheep to pass. While wandering through the village, give them a wide berth. If sheep are on the sidewalk, take to the grass.

Goathland—Site 46

- **Do not approach the sheep**. If they approach you, walk away.

- **If the village sheep seem to be begging for tidbits, they probably are.** Goathland sheep are tourist savvy and expect you to be an easy touch. **Do not feed them**. Walk away.

- **Watch where you walk!** Sheep deposit dung willy-nilly, hither and thither, often on paved lanes and steps. Step over it.

[©2009 Tara Bellers]

The Goathland Railway Station
http://www.goathlandstation.org.uk/
http://en.wikipedia.org/wiki/North_Yorkshire_Moors_Railway

Goathland Station is part of the **North Yorkshire Moors Railway** (NYMR), a private charitable trust dedicated to preserving England's railroad history. The NYMR is the second-longest heritage railway in Britain and carries up to 250,000 passengers a year. Most NYMR trains are steam-powered, with vintage diesel engines used for special events.

In 1836, Goathland's original station was located at the top of an incline on Beck Hole Road, north of the Village Green. The current station, where Harry Potter (and *Heartbeat*) filming took place, opened in 1865. It is just west of the Village Green, and down the hill.

Station facilities include:
- Tea Room
- Gift Shop
- Booking Office
- Waiting Room
- Toilets

Harry Potter Places Book Four

Goathland Station facilities are only open when the station is in operation—a schedule that varies from day to day, month to month. Happily, because all *Sorcerer's Stone* filming took place outside the station, access to station facilities isn't absolutely necessary. However, Goathland Station Potter Pix are best taken **while a train is at the station**, and the Gift Shop sells railway souvenirs that may be of interest.

Trains run to and from Goathland Station almost every day from April to October. During other months, they run on weekends and selected holidays. On some days, trains begin arriving as early as 9:45am, with the last departure at 6:45pm. Other days, trains run only between 10:50am and 4:50pm. During the summer, trains usually arrive and depart Goathland Station once each hour.

To learn when the station will be open during your visit, go to the **NYMR website**, mouse-on the **Timetables & Fares** tab, and select **Timetable**.
http://www.nymr.co.uk/

The Railway in Wartime

Each year, on three days over one weekend in October, an enormously popular special event is held at stations along the line, **Wartime Weekend**.
http://www.nymr.co.uk/special-events/the-railway-at-war/

Wartime Weekend is a celebration of UK railway operation during the Second World War. All NYMR stations are decorated to appear as they would during WWII wartime: sandbags are piled around entrances, windows are taped up, and station names are covered. Professional and amateur period re-enactors attend in 1940s military or civilian costume, adding to the authenticity and ambience. Street parades, battle reenactments, and memorabilia sellers abound. Vintage WWII civilian and military vehicles—**including *tanks***—rumble over the roads leading to and from the NYMR stations.

[©2008 C.D. Miller]

Goathland—Site 46

The popularity of Wartime Weekend cannot be overstated. Hoards of Muggles, young and old, flock to all the villages served by the NYMR, overloading every lodging accommodation available. If you'll be Pottering to Goathland in **October**, be sure to check the NYMR website for the Wartime Weekend dates. Unless you can book your lodgings 6 months or more in advance, you may not find a nearby place to stay during that weekend.

Still, visiting Goathland during Wartime Weekend is wonderful fun. In addition to enjoying all the WWII vehicles and trappings, Potter Pix containing people in vintage costumes are particularly special.

[©2008 C.D. Miller]

Goathland Station as Hogsmead Station

The very first scenes ever filmed for a Harry Potter movie were shot at Goathland Station!

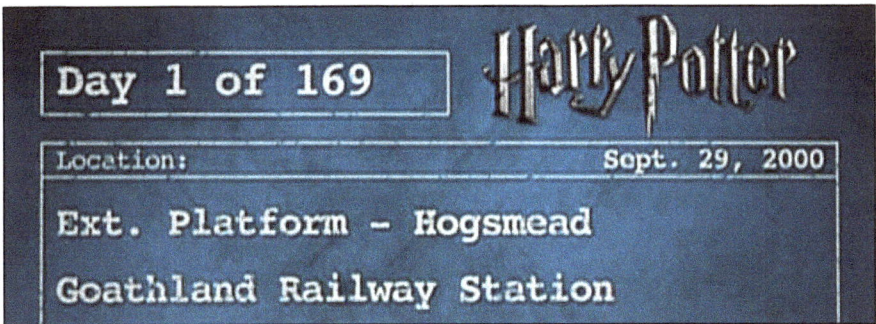

[*Sorcerer's Stone* Ultimate Edition screenshot segment (enhanced)]

Oddly enough, the first Harry Potter scenes ever shot were the *last* scenes seen on screen in the first Harry Potter movie: Hagrid saying farewell to Harry, Ron, and Hermione at Hogsmeade Station—as they boarded Hogwarts Express to head home *after* their first year at school.

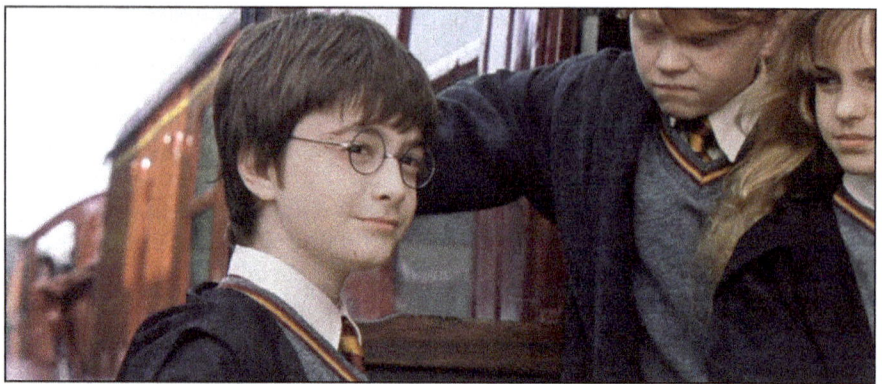

[*Sorcerer's Stone* screenshot (enhanced)]

"I'm not going home—not really."

Then, on the evening of the first filming day, scenes of the Trio's first arrival at Hogsmeade Station were shot.

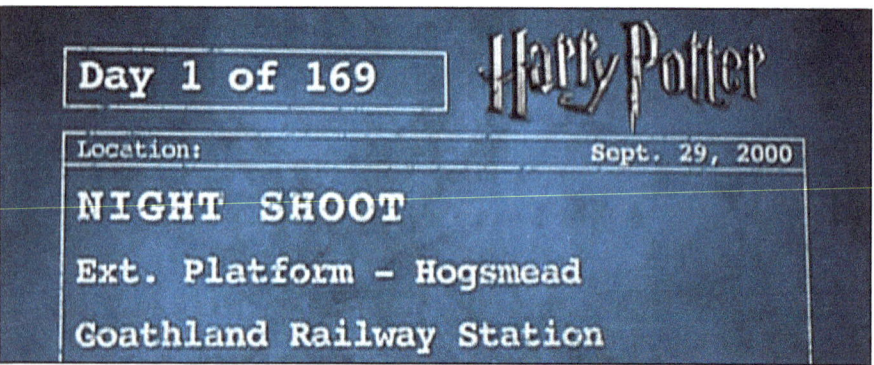

[*Sorcerer's Stone* Ultimate Edition screenshot segment (enhanced)]

Given the unique distinction of being the first Harry Potter film site, and the first Hogsmead Station location, Goathland is a **must see place** for Potterites traveling beyond London, by train or car.

Goathland—Site 46

Goathland Potter Pix

Goathland Potter Pic #1 is the Weasley Flying Ford Anglia—Wherever You Find It

[*Chamber of Secrets* screenshot segment (enhanced)]

While you'll not be able to recreate screenshots with stand-ins posing *inside* the car, beside-the-car pix are **Potterrific.**

All other Goathland Potter Pix are Hogsmead Station pix and best shot while a train is present. The first three station screenshots are daytime scenes from *Sorcerer's Stone*.

Goathland Potter Pix #2 and #3

[*Sorcerer's Stone* screenshots (enhanced) above and below]

63

Goathland Potter Pic #4

After you've snapped Pix #2 and #3, go over the bridge leading to the opposite platform, turn left and head to the northern end. There you'll find some steps leading to a gate on your right, with a grassy hillside stairway beyond.

If no train is present, you can walk across the tracks to the gate, via the path immediately in front of the Station-side platform's entrance/exit.

[©2009 Tara Bellers]

Instead of going up the hillside, turn left and walk along the inclined fence as far as you can. From there you should have the height needed to take a pic very similar to the next screenshot. If that spot isn't quite high enough, take the grassy stairs up the hillside and snap from there.

Goathland—Site 46

[*Sorcerer's Stone* screenshot (enhanced)]

Obviously, you'll not have Hogwarts Castle in the background. But the station's platforms, platform buildings, and the red bridge exist in real-life.

The final four Goathland Potter Pix are night scenes of the first time Harry, Ron, and Hermione arrived at Hogsmeade Station. These *Sorcerer's Stone* screenshots (enhanced) can be recreated during the daytime—and *should be*, just in case it's not dark when the last train passes through. Potterites lodging in Goathland can return and also snap nighttime recreation pix.

Goathland Potter Pic #5

Goathland Potter Pic #6

Goathland Potter Pic #7

Goathland Potter Pic #8

Goathland—Site 46

Nearby Potter Places

Goathland is a great place to stay on your way north to the other two **Great Site NEWTs**: **Durham Cathedral** (Site #45) and **Alnwick Castle** (Site #44).
- Drive time from Goathland to Durham Cathedral is approximately 1 hour 45 minutes.

- Drive time from Durham Cathedral to Alnwick Castle is approximately 1 hour 10 minutes.

If you arrive in Goathland early on an afternoon, visit and overnight there, you can head for Durham Cathedral bright and early the next morning, Pottering to Alnwick Castle in the afternoon. For Potterites continuing to **Scotland**, *eight* Potter Places are found in **Edinburgh** (Part One of *Harry Potter Places* Book Five—Scotland: Hogwarts' Home), which is only a 2-hour drive north from Alnwick Castle.

Lodging Options

Check in Cheap: Goathland Area Hostels

The closest Hostel is in **Whitby**, only a 20 minute drive from Goathland. Visit the **Youth Hostels Association (England & Wales)** website:
http://www.yha.org.uk/

For Region, select **Yorkshire**. For YHA location, select **Whitby**.

Board at the Burrow: Goathland Guest Houses, Bed & Breakfast Establishments

Fairhaven Country Guesthouse
http://www.fairhavencountryguesthouse.co.uk/

Free WiFi Internet access.

CD Miller stayed here in October of 2008:
> "This is a lovely home, run by very helpful and friendly folk, and is less than a block away from the Goathland Village Green shops. My room was quite comfortable, and breakfast was delicious. I'd stay here again!"

Please Note: Miller's solo October 2008 trip was planned in August, and her Goathland visit was accidentally scheduled over Wartime Weekend. She found a bed to book there only because most Wartime Weekenders are *couples*, and the Fairhaven's **single bedroom** was still available.

Glendale House
http://www.glendalehouse.co.uk/

The Glendale House website is the *most helpful* Goathland information resource on the Internet. They offer webpages about *Heartbeat* and *Harry Potter*, as well as Wartime Weekend, Steam Trains, other area events—even Goathland-related **Captain Cook** information.

The proprietors, Keith and Sandra Simmonds, are particularly Potter-friendly Goathlanders, who can regale you with stories about their personal experiences during the filming of *Sorcerer's Stone*. For instance:

> "When the Warner Bros. circus rolled into town to begin filming for Harry Potter, they needed help with some of the costumes and asked if anyone could sew. When they weren't overwhelmed with volunteers, Sandra agreed to help, along with two of her friends. What was supposed to be only a couple hours of work turned out to take all week. They sewed Hogwarts badges on all the school uniforms and adjusted Robbie Coltrane's outfit. As one of our friends keeps telling people, 'Sandra has had her hand in Robbie Coltrane's trousers!'"

Glendale House is the last house before you round the corner and arrive at the Goathland Village Green shops. All rooms are ensuite with Free WiFi Internet access.

The Leaky Cauldron to Malfoy Manor: Livable to Luxurious Goathland Hotels

Goathland Hotel
http://www.thegoathlandhotel.co.uk/

For 18 years, the Goathland Hotel prominently appeared in *Heartbeat* as the **Aidensfield Arms** hotel. Located directly across the street from the Goathland Garage and Antique Shop (aka, Aidensfield Garage and Scripps Funeral Services), this is the lodging option closest to Goathland's Railway Station.

A WiFi signal is unavailable and Trip Advisor reviews of the Goathland Hotel are not particularly positive. However, Tara Bellers stayed here in July of 2009, finding it "comfortable and super-convenient."

Inn on The Moor Hotel & Holiday Cottages
http://www.gv11r.co.uk/

WiFi available only in some rooms.

Mallyan Spout Hotel
http://www.mallyanspout.co.uk/

Free WiFi Internet access.

Goathland—Site 46

For additional accommodation options in and near Goathland, visit Trip Advisor:
http://www.tripadvisor.co.uk/Hotels-g1096363-Goathland_North_Yorkshire_England-Hotels.html

Going to Goathland
 Public Transportation

Use the **Transport Direct** website to plan your journey:
http://www.transportdirect.info/

Your destination is **Goathland (North Yorkshire Moors Railway)**.

🚗 Driving to Goathland

SatNav/GPS: Goathland, North Yorkshire, YO22 5NF

The coordinates above are for the Railway Station. Using a post code to find your Goathland lodgings will be problematic, as many Goathland Guest Houses and Hotels share the same post code. If you'll be staying at **Glendale House**, they have a marvelous aerial photo on their website that shows exactly where they are. Otherwise, watch for your lodgings' sign while driving through the village enroute to the Railway Station's coordinates.

If you'll not be lodging in Goathland, a large public car park is just past the Village Green shops. After rounding the bend before the Village Green shops, turn left (north) on **Beck Hole Road** and look to your left. Public toilets are in the small hut at the north end of the lot.

47

Hardwick Hall
Derbyshire

Malfoy Manor
http://www.nationaltrust.org.uk/hardwick/
http://en.wikipedia.org/wiki/Hardwick_Hall
http://www.english-heritage.org.uk/daysout/properties/hardwick-old-hall/
http://www.timetravel-britain.com/articles/houses/hardwick.shtml

Google Maps UK: Hardwick Hall, Doe Lea, Chesterfield, Derbyshire S44 5QJ

★Please Note: SatNav/GPS device directions can be problematic. See our **Driving to Hardwick Hall** section.

Visit Time: Schedule at least one hour to snap Potter Pix before going to your next site. Schedule two hours to include the gift shop and snack kiosk. Scheduling three or more hours here will afford time for leisurely pic-snapping while touring the manor and the ruins, as well as gift shopping and enjoying a sip or sup at the brand new Great Barn restaurant within the newly-restored Hardwick Stableyard buildings.

Photography *is* allowed inside Hardwick Hall with *!!!Flash OFF!!!*

Parseltongue Pointers:
- Derbyshire = "DAR-bee-sher"
- Shrewsbury = "SHROWZ-bree" or (locally) "SHREWZ-bree"

Hardwick Hall is considered one of the finest Elizabethan houses in all of Britain, and is one of the earliest examples of the English Renaissance architectural style that came into fashion when it was no longer thought necessary to *fortify* one's home with impenetrable walls. The hall's design and construction was ordered and overseen by **Elizabeth Talbot, Dowager Countess of Shrewsbury**—aka, **Bess of Hardwick**—between 1590 and 1597.

Born the daughter of a simple country Squire, the story of Elizabeth Talbot's rise to become the wealthiest and most powerful woman in England (second only to Queen Elizabeth I—who became a personal friend) is extraordinary. Bess survived four marriages, eight births, a seven-month imprisonment in the Tower of London, and numerous court intrigues. (At one point, Bess was even the "keeper" of Mary Queen of Scots.)

Bess of Hardwick's history is thoroughly entertaining. Below are our favorite free information sources.
http://en.wikipedia.org/wiki/Bess_of_Hardwick
http://www.tudorplace.com.ar/Bios/BessofHardwick.htm

Before 1597, when she took up residence in her newly completed Hardwick Hall, Bess lived in **Hardwick Old Hall**—a structure she had built several years earlier. Hardwick Old Hall is located little more than 300 feet southwest of the new Hall. At the center of these 16th century ruins you can visit the 14th century remains of the modest country manor where Elizabeth Talbot was born in 1527.

Hardwick Hall is most renowned for the vast number and enormous size of its **glass windows**, something quite unusual for the 16th century, when glass was considered an extravagance. Locals expressed their awe of the place in rhyming couplet: "Hardwick Hall, more glass than wall." People especially marveled when all its windows were lit up at night, making Hardwick Hall look like "a Giant's Lantern set on a hill."

For several hundred years after her death, Bess' descendants, particularly the **Dukes of Devonshire**, painstakingly maintained and improved Hardwick Hall. The collection of 16th and 17th century furnishings on display is surpassed only by the phenomenal **Hardwick Hall Textile Collection**. Considered the largest number of tapestries, canvas-works, and other textiles to have been created and privately preserved by a single family, the Hardwick textile collection also boasts the largest number of embroidery works ever created by and for one household. Many of the embroideries are Bess' needlework.

Hardwick Hall remained the private property of Elizabeth Talbot's descendants until 1956, when the family was unable to pay its Estate Duty and forfeited the property to the **Treasury of England**. Three years later, the Treasury transferred Hardwick Hall's ownership to the **National Trust**, to ensure its continued preservation as a national treasure.

Hardwick Hall as Malfoy Manor

The **Harry Potter Wikia** website has a wonderful page dedicated to **Malfoy Manor**. There you'll find examples of JK Rowling's Malfoy Manor

Hardwick Hall—Site 47

descriptions; info about a Malfoy Manor scene that was planned for *Chamber of Secrets* or *Goblet of Fire*, but never appeared on screen (or DVD); some interior set concept art; and a few Malfoy Manor screenshots.
http://harrypotter.wikia.com/wiki/Malfoy_Manor

Malfoy Manor is first seen in one of the **Special Features** found on the ***Order of the Phoenix* Two-Disc Special Edition DVD**, released in December of 2007: *"The Hidden Secrets of Harry Potter."* It appears in a portrait mounted on the wall behind Lucius Malfoy, who is ostentatiously posing beside a Malfoy Manor fireplace.

[*Order of the Phoenix* Special Features screenshot (enhanced)]

Oddly enough, it wasn't until 2009 that a Harry Potter film crew visited and shot exterior footage—both by helicopter and from the ground—for the purpose of using Hardwick Hall as Malfoy Manor in *Deathly Hallows*. The crew also photographed and measured several rooms *inside* the Hall, to use as reference and inspiration for Malfoy Manor **interior set designs**.

[©2011 Tara Bellers] [*Deathly Hallows* trailer screenshot segment (enhanced)]

Harry Potter Places Book Four

When both structures are seen side-by-side, it is clear that Hardwick Hall's towers and central range were merely topped with CGI spires to create Malfoy Manor.

[*Deathly Hallows Part 1* screenshot segment (enhanced)]

Additionally, within footage of Professor Snape's aerial approach to Malfoy Manor, the discerning Potterite eye can spy **ruins** of an *older* **Malfoy Manor** in the same relative location as the Hardwick Old Hall ruins found southwest of Hardwick Hall.

😐 Hardwick Hall is Assigned a Might-be-Fun Rating Because:

• The exterior of Hardwick Hall is clearly recognizable as Malfoy Manor.

• However, even though reference footage filmed within *inspired* aspects of Malfoy Manor interior set design, **only a single screenshot can actually be reproduced inside Hardwick Hall.**

• **The only reasonably convenient way to reach Hardwick Hall is to drive there.** The Estate is somewhat centrally-located between four other Potter Places, thus at least one other site can be enjoyed on a Hardwick Hall visit day.

• **Hardwick Hall is *not* a convenient trip via public transportation.** Journeying here will require several hours of train *and* bus travel, followed by a **2 mile walk** or a pricey **Taxi ride**. Furthermore, you'll not have time to Potter about any *other* site on the same day.

☹️ Potterites who aren't touring by car should *skip* Hardwick Hall.

Hardwick Hall—Site 47

Hardwick 2012 Operation Hours and Entry Fees

While both halls at Hardwick are owned by the **National Trust**, only Hardwick Hall is *run* by the Trust. Hardwick Old Hall is operated by the **English Heritage** organization. Check both of their websites to discover operation hours in effect during your visit, and obtain up-to-date entry fee and event information.

Hardwick Old Hall 2012 Operation Hours and Entry Fees
http://www.english-heritage.org.uk/daysout/properties/hardwick-old-hall/prices-and-opening-times

- April 1st to November 4th, open from 10am to 5pm on Wednesdays through Sundays, closed on Mondays and Tuesdays.

- November 2012 through March 2013, open only on weekends from 10am to 4pm.

Entry Fees: Adults £5 ($8), Children £3 ($5), Seniors and Students £4.50 ($7), Family £13 ($21).

The English Heritage organization also sells Joint Halls & Garden tickets, but doesn't offer the **Gift Aid Admission** option (explained below).

Hardwick Hall 2012 Operation Hours
http://www.nationaltrust.org.uk/hardwick/opening-times/

This schedule varies throughout the year. In general, Hardwick Hall is open from 12pm to 4:30pm on Wednesdays through Sundays, and Bank Holidays, between mid-February and the end of October. The Hall is closed in November, January, and early February. During other months, it is open from 11am to 3pm on weekends only.

2012 Hardwick Garden, Restaurant and Shop Operation Hours

In April of 2012, the £6.5 million **Stableyard** project that had been under development for seven years was completed.

> "The **Great Barn**, once the centre of agricultural activity on the Hardwick Estate, has been converted into a contemporary and stylish two-storey restaurant. Visitors will be able to enjoy a long lunch with friends or indulge in a quick coffee and bacon sandwich with the morning's paper … A further food outlet, the **Coach House Kiosk**, serves delicious light snacks and ice-cream and is ideal for packing a quick picnic to take with you on a stroll in the parkland … [The] **Stables Shop** is stocked with a selection of hand-picked and high-quality gifts and the Outdoors and **Garden Shop** is packed full with gardening gear and plants, including some grown on the Hardwick estate."

Harry Potter Places Book Four

From April through December of 2012, these facilities are scheduled to be open from 9am to 6pm, every day of the week.

Hardwick 2012 Entry Fees

A **Gift Aid Admission Ticket** costs 10% more than a **Standard Ticket**—representing a **voluntary 10% donation to the National Trust**. But, because the National Trust can reclaim the tax on the *whole* amount paid for the ticket, this small donation ends up being worth far more than merely 10% of the Standard ticket price. In the list below, the first amount is the Gift Aid ticket price, the second is the Standard price. **Paying the Gift Aid price is a Potterly Polite thing to do**.

Hardwick Hall and Garden: Adults £11.50/£10.45 ($18/$17), Children under 16 years old £5.80/£5.27 ($9/$8), Family £28.80/£26.18 ($46/$42).

Joint Halls and Garden: Adults £15/£14 ($24/$22), Children under 16 years old £7.50/£7 ($12/$11), Family £37.50/£35 ($59/$55).

Garden Only: Adults £5.80/£5.27 ($9/$8), Children under 16 years old free.

Hardwick Hall Tours

> "Tours and talks run throughout open season - please check at the Gatehouse or ring 01246 858400"

If a full tour of the manor isn't available on your visit day, no problem. Volunteer Hardwick Hall **Room Guides** can provide historical information at almost every turn.

Hardwick Hall Potter Pix

Malfoy Manor Potter Pic #1

[©2011 Tara Bellers] [*Deathly Hallows* trailer screenshot segment (enhanced)]

Take photos of Hardwick Hall's front face as you approach from the Great Gate entrance. Pix of you and others in your party snapped while standing in front of Malfoy Manor will also be fun.

Hardwick Hall—Site 47

Malfoy Manor Potter Pic #2

The lane traversed by Professor Snape—as well as by Scabior & the Death Eaters, when delivering Harry, Ron, and Hermione to the Malfoys—is closely flanked by tall, sharply-manicured hedges.

[*Deathly Hallows Part 1* screenshot (enhanced)]

The lane leading to the south side of Hardwick Hall, from the center of its **Formal Gardens**, is also closely flanked by tall, sharply-manicured hedges.

[©2011 Tara Bellers]

Malfoy Manor Potter Pix #3 and 4

The following screenshot contains aspects similar to portions of *two* locations within Hardwick Hall—hence, two Potter Pic numbers, but only one screenshot.

Please remember that only ***!!!Flash OFF!!!*** photography is allowed inside Hardwick Hall in order to preserve the priceless paintings and textiles.

Be very careful to avoid accidental flashing so as to also **preserve interior photography permission for future Potterites**.

The Hardwick Hall **Long Gallery** (aka, the **Portrait Gallery**) is the largest of all surviving Elizabethan Long Galleries in the UK. Its fireplace has a *single* oval stone sculpture section above its mantel. The Malfoy Manor **Entrance Hall set** fireplace has a large and elaborate overmantel with *two* oval stone sculptures. Unfortunately, that's the full extent of similarity between these two fireplaces.

Yes, we're stretching! But, after having traveled so far, we want to help you enjoy every possible Potter Pic opportunity that can be found at Hardwick Hall.

[*Deathly Hallows Part 1* screenshot (enhanced)]

The steps of Hardwick Hall's **Great Staircase** look strikingly similar to the **disturbing steps** seen in the Malfoy Manor Entrance Hall screenshot above. To fully reveal the similarity, however, a photo of the real-life Hardwick Great Staircase must be *inverted*.

[*DHp1* screenshot segment (enhanced)] [©2011 Tara Bellers]

Hardwick Hall—Site 47

Inversion of Tara's Great Staircase pic also reveals why Malfoy Manor Entrance Hall set steps are so **disturbing** to look at—they really are *upside-down* steps!

Malfoy Manor Potter Pic #5

Hardwick's **Great Hall** contains a long and slender, dark oak table and benches dating from the Elizabethan age, positioned parallel to a grand fireplace with a stone-carved overmantel featuring the coat of arms designed for Elizabeth, Countess of Shrewsbury.

At one end of the Great Hall are four classical stone columns that support an overhead Gallery, where musicians once accompanied Bess's opulent dinner parties. The two middle columns—situated directly behind the head of the long table—are mounted on a common stone plinth.

[©2011 Tara Bellers]

Have a Voldemort stand-in kneel between the table and plinth to snap **the *only* screenshot that can reasonably be reproduced *inside* Hardwick Hall.**

[*Deathly Hallows Part 1* screenshot (enhanced)]

Harry Potter Places Book Four

Malfoy Manor Potter Pix #6 and #7

The Malfoy Manor Great Hall fireplace overmantel looks *nothing* like the one in Hardwick's Great Hall. And, although Malfoy Manor's Elizabethan table is made of dark oak, it is flanked by *chairs* rather than benches. Yet, below are two *DHp1* screenshots that you can snap *somewhat similar* Potter Pix of while visiting Hardwick's Great Hall.

[*Deathly Hallows Part 1* screenshots (enhanced) above and below]

🛏 Lodging Options

Hardwick Hall is a between-site foray. Explore lodgings at the site you'll reach at the end of your Malfoy Manor visit day.

Going To Hardwick Hall
Public Transportation

Visiting Hardwick Hall via public transportation will take almost an entire day and is quite complicated. Obtaining travel information and bookings for your requires the use of **Train, Bus, and Taxi** (or a healthy walk).

Hardwick Hall—Site 47

🚆 **Step 1: Chesterfield Railway Station** (**CHD**) is the train station nearest to Hardwick Hall. Use the **National Rail** website to plan the route **from your departure point to CHD**.
http://www.nationalrail.co.uk/

🚌 **Step 2:** Use the **Transport Direct** website to obtain directions for the bus portion of your journey.
http://www.transportdirect.info

- From **Chesterfield** (Station/airport).
- To **Glapwell, Derbyshire** (Town/district/village).
- Follow Transport Direct's instructions for reaching the Bus Station where you can catch the **Pronto Bus**. Disembark at the **Glapwell, Young Vanish (on the Hill)** Bus Stop.

Please Note: Although **Google Maps UK** images show Bus Stop icons on the lane in front of **Hardwick Old Hall**, this is an **error**. No public busses can take you anywhere within the Hardwick Estate.

TAXI **Step 3:** To take a **Taxi** from the Glapwell Pronto Bus Stop to Hardwick Hall, pop across the street to the **Young Vanish Inn and Carvery**. Order a beverage and ask your server to call a cab for you.

Please Note: While some Taxi drivers may insist otherwise, in reality it could take **up to an hour** for them to respond to a pick-up call placed from Hardwick Hall. Be sure to arrange a **return pick-up** *appointment* with your driver.

🚶 **Step 3 Alternative:** Walk 2 miles (45 minutes) to Hardwick Hall.

If you have a **Smartphone**, the English Heritage website offers a **Days Out** download for iPhone and Android. It includes all of their properties and will generate a map and directions for you.
http://www.english-heritage.org.uk/daysout/app/

Use **Google Maps UK** to obtain walking directions.
- Search for **United Kingdom (Glapwell, Young Vanish (adj))** [Notice the *two* end-parenthesis after "adj."]

- Click on the **down-chevron** next to "Glapwell, Young Vanish (adj)," then click on **Directions**.

- Switch "Glapwell, Young Vanish (adj)" to the **A** box.

- Click on the 🚶 icon.

- Insert "**Hardwick Hall, Doe Lea, Chesterfield, Derbyshire S44 5QJ**" into the **B** box.

Harry Potter Places Book Four

- Click on **Get Directions**.

- Select the "**Rowthorne Lane**" route option—it's a far shorter walk.

🚗 Driving to Hardwick Hall

SatNav/GPS Coordinates: Hardwick Hall, Doe Lea, Chesterfield, Derbyshire S44 5QJ

If you have a **Smartphone**, the English Heritage website offers a **Days Out** download for iPhone and Android (weblink above). They also offer **Tom Tom** or **Garmin** SatNav/GPS downloads.
http://www.english-heritage.org.uk/daysout/satnav/

The Hardwick Estate is centrally-located when traveling *between* the following Potter Places:

- **Oxford** (*Harry Potter Places Book Two—OWLs: Oxford Wizarding Locations*) and **Malham Cove** (Site #48)

- **Oxford** and **Goathland Station** (Site #46)

- **Malham Cove** and **Goathland Station**

- **Malham Cove** and **Lavenham** (a London Side-Along Apparation, Site #19, found in *Harry Potter Places Book One*)

*The Hardwick Hall SatNav/GPS Conundrum:

Shortly after leaving the **M1 Motorway at Junction (exit)** #29—the exit you'll need to take whether heading to Hardwick from the south *or* the north—your SatNav/GPS device may deliver directions that will send you the **wrong way** along the **one-way**, **single-lane road** that leads through the Hardwick Estate Park.

Use the SatNav/GPS coordinates above to reach the M1 Junction #29. Then, follow your device's directions to **exit the M1**, navigate the roundabout leading to **the A6175**, and to **turn left onto Mill Lane** to begin driving southeast.

At that point, turn to the Driving Directions we provide below. Happily, after you've *deviated* from your SatNav/GPS device's directions and passed under the M1 (heading toward **Stainsby Mill**), your device should *update* and give you correct prompts. Ignore any cues to "turn around" until it does.

If you've passed Stainsby Mill and the SatNav/GPS device still hasn't updated your route directions, turn it off and continue to follow our Driving Directions.

Hardwick Hall—Site 47

🚘 Driving Directions *to* Hardwick Hall

When driving southeast on **Mill Lane**, watch on your left for a brown sign directing you to turn left to reach **Ault Hucknall / Hardwick Hall / Stainsby Mill**. ♦ Turn left and drive east, **passing under the M1**, and continue to the lane's end. (Keep *left* at the lane-end fork—you're driving in the UK!) ♦ Turn right at the lane's end and drive south, passing **Stainsby Mill**.

Keep left at the next fork, but do *not* cross the bridge and drive east on **Hodmire Lane** (see below). Instead, **turn right** just before the bridge, and then immediately **turn left** to resume driving south, and enter the **Hardwick Estate grounds**.

[Google Maps UK Streetview segment (enhanced) ©2009 Google]

Follow the Estate lane south as it curves east, then back south again. ♦ When you reach the **T-intersection**, turn right to head southwest. You'll spy Hardwick Hall in the distance, on the left side of the new lane. ♦ When you reach a small gate with a livestock grate, you may or may not see a little wooden **Queen's-Guard-like hut** on your right. [In addition to the newly-restored Stables opening, Hardwick Hall Car Park renovation was completed in April of 2012. We don't know what it looks like today. (**Google Maps UK**'s Streetview images date from 2009.)]

The car park entrance should be approximately a block ahead, on your left. After parking, look for the **Century Box** to pay your **£2 ($3) Car Park Fee**.

Walk south from the car park to reach Hardwick Hall's **Great Gate** visitor entrance. The Hardwick Old Hall ruins are just beyond the Great Gate.

🚘 Leaving Hardwick Hall

After enjoying Hardwick, program your SatNav/GPS device with your next destination's coordinates. If your device leads you **south** from the car park (past the Great Gate, and past Hardwick Old Hall's ruins), **follow its directions.** If not, follow our Driving Directions below.

Harry Potter Places Book Four

🚗 Driving Directions *from* Hardwick Hall

Leave the car park. ♦ Turn left and drive south, passing the Hardwick Hall Great Gate and the Hardwick Old Hall ruins. ♦ When you pass the **Hardwick Stone Centre**, the road curves west. ♦ Just beyond the south gate of Hardwick Estate's grounds, you'll see the **Hardwick Inn** on your left. After passing the Inn's car park, the road curves northwest. ♦ At the next fork, keep right (in the left lane) to continue northwest toward **Motorway / Stainsby Heath / Hardwick Hall / Stainsby Mill**.

After driving **under the M1 Motorway**, the road curves north. Continue north until you reach a fork in the road. ♦ Keep right to continue north on **Mill Lane** as it curves northwest, until you reach the **A6175**. ♦ Turn right and drive northeast on the A6175.

At this point, you can resume following directions from your SatNav/GPS device.

48

MALHAM COVE

A *Deathly Hallows Part One* Campsite
http://www.malhamdale.com
http://en.wikipedia.org/wiki/Malham_Cove

Google Maps UK: 54.070833, -2.158611

Operation Hours and Entry Fee: None. But, do *not* begin your hike to the Limestone Pavement film site less than 2 hours before sunset—no matter which route you use to get there.

Visit Dates: Avoid visiting Malham Cove between November and March. Icy rains or heavy snowfalls may occur with little warning during those months, seriously endangering any hiker in the area.

Visit Time: If you'll not be overnighting in the village, schedule **no less than 2 hours** for your Malham visit. That time frame allows 40 minutes to reach the film site (you'll need to hustle), 40 minutes to visit the film site, and 40 minutes to return to where you parked. Scheduling **3 hours** in Malham will afford a more leisurely hike, and also give you time to enjoy a sip or sup at the Lister Arms Hotel (where *DHp1* cast and crew lodged).

Parseltongue Pointers:
- Malham = "MAL-um"
- Pennine Way = "PEN-NINE way" (not "pen-neen")
- Yorkshire = "YORK-sher"

In 1954, an area of 680 square miles (1,770 square kilometers) was designated as the **Yorkshire Dales National Park** (YDNP). A section of the **Pennine Way**—an ancient National Trail in England—runs through the YDNP. And, over 20,000 people live and work within the many towns and villages located within the YDNP.
http://www.yorkshiredales.org.uk/

Harry Potter Places Book Four

http://en.wikipedia.org/wiki/Yorkshire_Dales
http://www.thepennineway.co.uk/
http://en.wikipedia.org/wiki/Pennine_Way

Just northwest of the YDNP village of **Malham,** part of the Pennine Way leads to a grand natural amphitheatre known as **Malham Cove.**

[©2011 Wolfgang Mletzko]

Atop the 260-foot-high cliffs that cradle Malham Cove is a remarkable **Limestone Pavement,** consisting of *clints* (small, relatively flat blocks) and *grikes* (the deep crevices between the clints)—a rock formation rarely seen anywhere else in the UK.

[©2011 Tara Bellers]

Malham Cove—Site 48

The unusual appearance of Malham Cove's limestone pavement is probably what attracted the eye of Harry Potter location scouts, and prompted its selection as a *Deathly Hallows Part One* campsite.

In November of 2009, *Deathly Hallows* cast and crew members moved into Malham village and lodged at the **Lister Arms Hotel**. Once filming was finished, cast members (Daniel Radcliffe and Emma Watson) departed. Thereafter, *DHp1* **background plate footage** was reportedly shot at three other nearby YDNP features of renown: **Malham Tarn**, **Gordale Scar**, and **Grassington Moor**.
http://en.wikipedia.org/wiki/Malham_Tarn
http://en.wikipedia.org/wiki/Gordale_Scar
http://www.grassington.uk.com/

Only the Limestone Pavement exterior camping scenes can be recognized in *DHp1* screenshots.

Malham Cove Scenes *Deathly Hallows Part One*

The morning after a horcrux-haunted Ron abandoned his companions in *DHp1*, Harry and Hermione disapparated to the Limestone Pavement atop Malham Cove and set up a new camp. While inside the tent pitched at this site, Harry took the Golden Snitch willed to him by Professor Dumbledore and put it to his lips, discovering the message, *"I open at the close!"*

Meanwhile, Hermione was perched upon a nearby limestone pavement clint when she realized that the strange symbol seen on a page in her copy of *The Tales of Beedle the Bard* was **drawn** there by someone—presumably Professor Dumbledore.

Site Rating

Malham Cove is Assigned a Might-be-Fun Rating Because:

- **This film site is not particularly convenient to reach.** For instance, it takes approximately 4 hours and 30 minutes to drive from **Oxford** (*Harry Potter Places Book Two—OWLs: Oxford Wizarding Locations*) directly to **Goathland** (Site #46). If you take a side-trip to **Malham** during that journey, your drive time increases to **6 hours and 30 minutes**. When you factor in the additional 2 to 3 hours required to Potter about *in* Malham, a journey between Oxford and Goathland that includes Malham will take **8 to 9½ hours**.

- The drive from **Oxford** directly to **Malham** is approximately **4 hours and 15 minutes**. But, if you must choose *between* visiting Malham or **Goathland**, Goathland is—by far—the preferred Potter Place to visit.

- After parking in Malham village, it's only a 15 to 30 minute walk to reach the base of Malham Cove's cliff face. Once there, however, you'll have to **climb up *400* irregular stone steps** to reach the Limestone Pavement film site.

[*Deathly Hallows Part 1* screenshot (enhanced)]

For Potterites who are driving and have plenty of holiday time:

- If you're in **good physical condition**, you'll find several distinctive *DHp1* screenshot reproduction opportunities after hiking to Malham Cove and climbing to the film site.

- If you're in *fairly*-**good physical condition**, you can hike a **Back-Way** we've discovered, and reach the film site *without* **having to climb up 400 irregular stone steps**. The road you'll be walking has only a few areas of steep grade, and the dirt path between the road and the limestone pavement is relatively level. However, the dirt path is unsigned, uneven, untended, and may be muddy.

😟 Potterites in poor physical condition should *skip* the Malham Cove film site. The Cove steps are arduous and the Back-Way route is remote.

Deathly Hallows Limestone Pavement Potter Pix

There are **15** (*fifteen*) wonderful screenshots that can be reproduced while visiting this *DHp1* film site! For Potterites wishing to see all of them, we created the ***Harry Potter Places* Malham Cove Limestone Pavement Screenshot Supplementum**.
http://www.HarryPotterPlaces.com/b4/MalhamScreenshots.pdf

For Potterites happy with merely **5** screenshot recreation options, our favorites are found below. All are *Deathly Hallows Part One* screenshots (en-

Malham Cove—Site 48

hanced). Pay close attention to the background vista when seeking the spot where any *DHp1* screenshot was filmed.

Limestone Pavement Potter Pic #1

Limestone Pavement Potter Pic #2

Limestone Pavement Potter Pic #3

Limestone Pavement Potter Pic #4

Limestone Pavement Potter Pic #5

Tips for Safe Pottering to the Limestone Pavement

No matter which route you use to reach the *DHp1* Limestone Pavement film site, as soon as you leave the road you'll be walking **out in the country**. The nearest rescue personnel are at least 14 miles away.

Malham Cove—Site 48

[Google Maps UK Streetview segment (enhanced) ©2009 Google]

Potterly Important Limestone Pavement Safety Pointers:
• **Whether or not you'll be tackling the 400 Malham Cove steps, wear proper hiking boots**. The limestone pavement is uneven and treacherous, especially when moist with dew, fog, or rain. Slips and falls here have resulted in wrist fractures and facial injuries. Even during perfectly dry conditions, trainers (tennis shoes)—or other soft-soled shoes—simply aren't safe enough for climbing up the Cove steps, or for Pottering on the precarious Limestone Pavement.

• Dress in layers no matter what time of year you are visiting, and bring a waterproof outer garment.

• Be sure that your cell phone is fully-charged.

• Pack high-calorie snacks and at least one bottle of water per person.

• Make sure that *someone*—such as your lodging hosts or Malham National Park Centre personnel—knows where you've gone hiking and approximately when you plan to return, especially if trekking the Back-Way route. Please avoid launching an unnecessary search and rescue mission by checking in again as soon as you safely return to civilization.

• To call for emergency help while Pottering anywhere in the UK, dial **999**.

Harry Potter Places Book Four

[©2011 Tara Bellers]

- If you'll be hiking the **Back-Way route**, pack a compass and a whistle. The sheep that live in the area tend to create extra paths willy-nilly. Although it's unlikely that you'll get lost, it's best to be prepared.

The Exclusive *Harry Potter Places* Back-Way Route

You'll not find mention of this route on any website or in any other travel guidebook—at least not until after *Harry Potter Places* Book Four is published. We devised our Limestone Pavement Back-Way directions after spending several hours using the **Google Maps UK** Streetview function to *virtually* explore the Malham area.

Then we checked our findings with Malham locals. (The Lister Arms and Buck Inn folks were very, very helpful.) Finally, Tara Bellers tested and *confirmed* our Back-Way route in July of 2011. She reports that it is a pleasant, comfortable walk and an easy route to follow.

Next, we created a collection of five **Google UK map** image sections—augmenting each to identify points and landmarks important to following our Back-Way route—and posted it on our website:
http://www.HarryPotterPlaces.com/b4/BackWayMaps.pdf

The only thing missing from our Back-Way Maps is the **directions** you'll find below!

Directions for the *Harry Potter Places* Back-Way Route

The **Lister Arms Hotel** is the start point for our Back-Way route. If you'll be lodging here, use the post code below to arrive at their car park.

SatNav/GPS: BD23 4DB

Malham Cove—Site 48

To reach the Lister Arms from elsewhere in Malham, follow our **Walk to the Malham Cove Limestone Pavement Film Site** directions, provided at the end of this chapter.

Refer to Back-Way Map 1 to Start Your Journey

🚶 **Point A:** Stand facing the street, with your back to the Lister Arms Hotel.
♦ Turn Left and walk northeast on **Finkle Street** for a few minutes, until you reach **Point B, Malham Rakes** (road). ♦ Turn left and walk northwest on Malham Rakes, keeping right to continue up the road as it curves north, northeast, then northwest again until you reach **Point C**.

Malham Rakes is a single-lane road flanked by stone fences. Whenever you reach a point where the road bends, be alert for motorists blindly approaching from either direction.

The distance between Points B and C is approximately ½ mile. Because portions of the road have a slightly steep grade, plan on a 20 to 30 minute walk between these points.

★**As you near Point C, you'll see a stone-rimmed TOR—a small hill—**to the left of the road ahead of you (pic below left). When you arrive at Point C, you'll see **sheep pens** between the road and the tor.

[©2011 Tara Bellers]

There are gates in the stone walls on either side of Point C. On the right (east side), is a small wooden gate sporting a sign that reads, "**Dogs Must Be Kept Under Close Control. Preferably on a Lead.**" Do not use that gate.

Instead, look beyond the large metal gate to the north on the **tor side** and you'll see a **narrow, wooden step ladder** straddling the stone fence on your left (pic below left). *Carefully* climb over the step ladder.

Harry Potter Places Book Four

[©2011 Tara Bellers]

The distance between Points C and D is ½ mile. Because the terrain is slightly rough and may be muddy, plan on a 20 to 30 minute walk.

★ **Before trekking across the sheep fields**, take a moment to review Back-Way Maps 2 and 3. Both are aerial views showing the country side and the plethora of paths found between Points C and D. **Yellow X**s mark the northwest and southeast corners of the **stone-fenced field** that is your **midway landmark**. Map 3 has a dotted red line indicating the route we suggest you take.

Please notice that the entire route between Points C and D is crisscrossed with lesser paths created by sheep and farm vehicles. Armed with our Back-Way Maps—with or without a compass— you shouldn't get lost.

Speaking of Sheep

When hiking between Points C and D you may encounter any number of sheep on or near the path. The pic below was shot by Tara while following our Back-Way route in July of 2011.

[©2011 Tara Bellers]

Malham Cove—Site 48

Stay *away* from the sheep!

Normally, sheep are docile creatures that flee when approached. However, if you unwittingly make a seemingly-sweet little sheep feel *threatened*, he or she **may charge you**. Ewes protecting newborn lambs are particularly prone to charging.

An eminent charge is usually prefaced by a few moments of aggressive head-on posturing and hoof-stamping. When faced with an aggressively hoof-stamping sheep, **immediately duck your head down** (discontinuing eye contact and assuming a submissive posture) and **move away**. Being head-butted by even a small sheep can cause plenty of unpleasant injuries.

Resuming Our Back-Way Directions

🚶 **Walk from Point C to Point D:** Head northwest on the path leading to the right of the tor. ♦ Near the tor's north end is a **fork in the path** (Back-Way Map 4, lower right corner). The **right fork** is more prominent and appears less rocky, which is why we suggest you follow that path. Happily, both paths leading from the tor fork converge at **the southeast corner of the stone-fenced field**. ♦ Whichever path you follow from the fork, walk to the southeast corner of the stone-fenced field.

🚶 **Continue toward Point D** (Back-Way Map 5). After reaching the field's southeast corner, walk along the stone-fence to its northwest corner. ♦ Then, follow the path that leads from that corner to Point D—a gateless opening in another stone fence.

[©2011 Tara Bellers]

Once through the opening, you'll be free to walk to Malham Cove's limestone pavement and search for places to take your Potter Pix.

Harry Potter Places BOOK FOUR

🚶 For Your Return Trip, Reverse the Back-Way Route

Because Malham Cove's 400 steps are so steep, narrow and uneven, Malham locals unanimously share the opinion that **walking *down* the Cove steps is even more dangerous than walking *up* them!** Do not walk down the Cove steps unless certain that you are physically capable of slowly and safely doing so.

Instead, trek back through the sheep fields to the tor. Turn right on Malham Rakes (road) and head back to the Lister Arms Hotel, where you should enjoy a well-deserved sip or sup.

The Malham Village Potter Place

[©2011 Tara Bellers]

The Lister Arms Hotel, Restaurant & Pub
http://listerarms.co.uk/

Address: 22 The Lane, Malham, Yorkshire BD23 4DB

Google Maps UK and SatNav/GPS: BD23 4DB

Do not use the Lister Arms address to map it on the Internet, or to program your SatNav/GPS device. That address may erroneously indicate a location far south of Malham, near the village of **Scosthrop**. Instead, use the Lister Arms' **post code**.

Please Note: A post code may also yield more accurate SatNav/GPS directions for other Malham accommodations.

In November of 2009, Harry Potter cast and crew members lodged at the **Lister Arms Hotel** while filming the *Deathly Hallows Part One* Limestone Pavement campsite scenes. Thus, Potterites who journey to Malham will enjoy visiting this establishment. If you can afford to lodge here, it wouldn't

Malham Cove—Site 48

hurt to ask if you can be booked into a room where Daniel Radcliffe or Emma Watson slept!

Situated in the center of Malham village, the Lister Arms Hotel is about a 20 minute walk from the Malham Cove cliff base (and the 400 steps)—as well as being the start point for our Back-Way route to the Limestone Pavement film site.

The Lister Arms is open year-round, 7 days a week, at 11am. Meals are served between noon and 9pm on Mondays through Saturdays, between noon and 8pm on Sundays. Menus, wine and beer lists, can be found on the Lister Arms' website. Teas, coffees, and a range of snacks are available to lodgers when the restaurant is closed.

All rooms at the Lister Arms Hotel are ensuite and offer free Wi-Fi Internet connection. 2012 nightly room rates include "a full Yorkshire breakfast" and range from £70 ($110) to £125 ($197), depending on the time of year and type of accommodation booked. Discounted rates are available for children up to 16 years old when staying with 2 adults.

A pet can be included in your advance reservation for an extra charge of only £15 ($24) per night, 10% of which is **donated to the Search and Rescue Dog Association**.

Laundry facilities are available for Lister Arms Hotel registered guests.

Parking is available for all registered guests.

A Non-Potter Place of Interest

The Malham National Park Centre
http://www.malhamdale.com/ydnp.htm

Google Maps UK and SatNav/GPS coordinates for the Centre are provided in the **Driving to Malham** section below.

Operation Hours: From April to October, the Centre is open between 9:30am and 5pm, 7 days a week. Winter operation hours vary from November to March.

Car Park: Fees are £2.50 ($4) for up to 2 hours, £4 ($6) for over 2 hours. Money collected from the Centre's car park is used to care for the **Yorkshire Dales National Park**.

The Malham National Park Centre is about a 30 to 40 minute walk from the Malham Cove cliff base, a 10 to 15 minute walk from the Back-Way start point.

In addition to standard tourist information such as local maps and **important daily weather forecasts**, the Centre offers a souvenir shop and an area of interactive displays that vividly illustrate the geological history of Malham Cove and its limestone pavement.

Harry Potter Places Book Four

Lodging Options
🛏 Check in Cheap: Malham Cove Area Hostels
The Malham Youth Hostel
http://www.yha.org.uk/hostel/malham

Address: Malham, Skipton, North Yorkshire BD23 4DB

Google Maps UK and SatNav/GPS: BD23 4DB

Operation Hours: The MYH reception desk is open every day of the year, from 7am to 10am, and from 5pm to 10:30pm.

Room Fees: Check the website (above) to obtain nightly tariff information during the dates of your holiday.

Situated just east of the Lister Arms Hotel, the **Malham Youth Hostel** (MYH) is a 20 to 30 minute walk from the Malham Cove cliff base—but is right next to the **start point of our Back-Way route to the Limestone Pavement film site**.

The MYH provides each lodger with clean bed linen and a pillow. Meals are available for purchase, and self-catered cooking facilities are provided free of charge.

The Hostel offers one washing machine and one drying machine, a drying rack room, bicycle and luggage storage. There also is some kind of shop on site.

The MYH has no Wi-Fi Internet access.

The Hostel parking lot has space for up to 15 cars.

The Hilltop Farm Bunk Barn
http://www.yorkshirenet.co.uk/ydales/bunkbarns/malham/

Address: Hill Top Farm, Malham, Skipton, North Yorkshire, BD23 4DJ

Google Maps UK and SatNav/GPS: BD23 4DJ

Hilltop Farm Bunk Barn is only a 10 minute walk from the Malham Cove cliff base.

Once used for hay storage and housing of cattle in the winter, the Hilltop Farm's barn was converted into a hostel-like lodging facility in 1986. Up to 32 people can be accommodated in 6 different-sized bedrooms, ranging from 2 to 11 beds in each.

The Bunk Barn charges only £15 ($25) per person per night, **but it doesn't rent *individual* beds on the weekends**. You'll have to book an entire room to stay here on the weekend—unless you're booking at the last minute and they happen to have an individual bed open.

Those who stay here must bring their own sleeping bags. No bed linens, blankets, or pillows are provided. No meals are served in the Bunk Barn,

Malham Cove—Site 48

but cooking facilities are available for preparing food brought with you. Toilets, showers, and a large drying rack room are offered, but there are no clothes washing or drying machines.

Wi-Fi is not available at the Bunk Barn.

Parking is available for approximately 8 cars.

⌂ Board at the Burrow: Malham Area Bed & Breakfast Establishments

To research the many Malham B&Bs available, as well as self-catering Malham accommodations, go to:
http://www.malhamdale.com/accom.htm

You can also peruse the **Trip Advisor** website to research Malham B&Bs:
http://www.tripadvisor.com/Hotels-g1076872-Malham_Yorkshire_Dales_National_Park_North_Yorkshire_England-Hotels.html

Use any Malham lodgings' **Post Code** for your **SatNav/GPS** coordinates.

⌂ The Leaky Cauldron to Malfoy Manor: Livable to Luxurious Malham Hotels

The Lister Arms

Please refer to the Lister Arms Hotel information provided above.

The Buck Inn
http://www.buckinnmalham.co.uk/

Address: The Buck Inn, Malham, Skipton, Yorkshire Dales BD23 4DA

Google Maps UK and SatNav/GPS: BD23 4DA

[©2011 Tara Bellers]

Built in 1874 on the site of an even older coaching inn, the **Buck Inn** is located about one mile from the Malham Cove cliff base (a 20 to 30 minute

Harry Potter Places Book Four

walk), and only 100 yards from the start of our Limestone Pavement film site Back-Way route.

The Buck Inn's nightly room rates include "a full English Breakfast," and, depending on the time of year and type of accommodation, range between £80 ($126) and £100 ($157) per night.

All rooms are ensuite with free Wi-Fi Internet connection

Parking is available for registered guests.

Going to Malham Cove

Public Transportation

Using public transportation to reach Malham will take significantly longer than the time required to drive here, but the village *can* be reached via train and bus. The best resource for Malham public transportation information is:
http://www.malhamdale.com/transport.htm

🚗 Driving to Malham

Please Note: Being a small country village, many of the roads leading to and from Malham are extremely narrow, and often have very poor visibility due to frequent bends and stone walls that closely-line *both* sides of the road. After rounding any bend you may suddenly encounter a slow-moving farm vehicle, walkers or cyclists, loose cattle or sheep or deer (oh my). Please drive slowly and with care.

Do Not Park on the side of *any* Malham country road. The cleared roadside verges you'll occasionally encounter are not parking places. They are intended to facilitate oncoming vehicle-passing (if the verge is on the *left*, **you** are supposed to pull over), or places that trucks and the like can use to turn around.

Furthermore, vehicles parked in remote locations are tempting targets for *thieves*. Please park only at your lodgings or in an officially recognized car park.

🚗 **Malham SatNav/GPS:** Chapel Gate, Malham, North Yorkshire BD23 4

The coordinates above lead to a spot just south of the **Malham National Park Centre**—the best place to park if you'll not be lodging in Malham.

As you approach Malham village from the south, the National Park Centre is the first building you'll see on your left. Turn left into the driveway to reach the Centre's car park.

After parking, purchase a **Pay-And-Display** ticket and follow directions for **where to place it**. Some UK P&D tickets must be placed on the dashboard, some must be stuck to the windscreen (windshield), some must be posted in the passenger-side window. Hefty fines will find you if you fail to correctly post a P&D ticket.

Malham Cove—Site 48

🚶 You may be able to walk directly east from your parking place—cutting between or through one of the buildings that line the east side of the Centre's car park—to reach **Chapel Gate** (road) and turn left to head for Malham Cove or the Back-Way route. However, it's probably best to first visit the National Park Centre and at least obtain **local weather information** before beginning your Limestone Pavement film site trek.

Walk to the Malham Cove Limestone Pavement Film Site

If you'll not be walking from the Malham National Park Centre, below is a link to a Malham map that clearly identifies the National Park Centre, the Youth Hostel, the Lister Arms Hotel, and many other Malham Village buildings. To follow our walking directions, you first must reach the triangular island seen just northeast of the Buck Inn.
http://www.yorkshiredales.org.uk/__data/assets/pdf_file/0010/224884/malham-4.pdf

🚶 When exiting the **Malham National Park Centre**, turn left and walk east to **Chapel Gate** (road). ♦ Turn left and walk north. ♦ As you pass the **Buck Inn** on your left, you'll see a **small, triangular grass island** that forms a **fork in the road** ahead.

🚶 To the Back-Way Limestone Pavement Route

Keep **right** at the triangular island to walk northeast on the lane leading over a stone bridge that crosses **Malham Beck stream**. ♦ Once past the bridge, watch on your left for the **Lister Arms Hotel**—the start point of our **Back-Way Limestone Pavement route**.

🚶 To the Malham Cove Pennine Way Trail Head (and 400 Steps)

Keep **left** at the triangular island to walk north on **Cove Road**, continuing as it curves west. ♦ When you see a sign on your left that reads, "**No Parking for 11 Miles**," look to your right for the **Pennine Way Trailhead** gate and enter. ♦ Follow the signs posted along that trail to find the 400 steps leading to the Limestone Pavement film site atop Malham Cove's cliffs.

49

NATIONAL RAILWAY MUSEUM

In York (Yorkshire) *or* **Shildon (County Durham)**
Home to Olton Hall—the *Hogwarts Express* Locomotive
http://www.nrm.org.uk/

Google Maps UK coordinates and visiting information is provided in the **Plan Your Visit** section.

☙❦❧

In September of 1975, **Prince Philip**, the Duke of Edinburgh and husband of **Queen Elizabeth II**, presided at the opening of the **National Railway Museum** (NRM) in **York**—the very first national museum ever located outside of London. Associated with Britain's **National Museum of Science and Industry**, the original NRM occupied a small group of buildings on Leeman Road, formerly known as the **York North Locomotive Depot**. Starting in 1990, the NRM began expanding into nearby properties.

In 2004, after an £11 million expenditure, an *annex* of the NRM was opened in **County Durham**, 60 miles north of York. **Locomotion: The National Railway Museum at Shildon** was the first national museum to be built in the north east.

Today, the NRM is one of Britain's busiest museums, its two locations attracting almost one million visitors each year. By *networking* with other heritage railways and rail museums across the UK, the National Railway Museum also has become **the largest railway museum in the world**.

The Olton Hall

[©2004 Dashwortley]

The **Olton Hall** is a Hall-class steam locomotive, bearing the number **5972**. Built in April of 1937 for the **Great Western Railway**, she was retired from service in December of 1963 and destined to become *scrap metal*. Instead (magically?), Olton Hall came to the attention of people interested in preserving steam locomotives. She was purchased by **West Coast Railways**, a privately-owned rail company that runs the **Jacobite** steam train between **Fort William** and Malaig, traversing the **Glenfinnan Viaduct** (see *Harry Potter Places* Book Five—Scotland: Hogwarts' Home, Sites #59 and #61).
http://www.westcoastrailways.co.uk/

[©2010 Tara Bellers]
(The full-sized Hogwarts Express replica at Florida's *Wizarding World of Harry Potter*)

National Railway Museum—Site 49

Magic struck again in 2000 when director Chris Columbus cast Olton Hall as the **Hogwarts Express locomotive** in *Harry Potter and the Sorcerer's Stone*. Since then, she has appeared in almost every Harry Potter movie.

To learn more about the Olton Hall, visit her Wikipedia webpage. But, beware the statement, "She is now based at the National Railway Museum in Shildon."
http://en.wikipedia.org/wiki/GWR_4900_Class_5972_Olton_Hall

Olton Hall is owned by West Coast Railways—*not* the NRM. Happily, WCR frequently *loans* her to the NRM. When on loan, Olton Hall may be exhibited at either of the museum's two locations. In the summer of 2010 she was briefly on display at NRM York, but in the summer of 2011 she was exhibited at NRM Shildon.

Additionally, because the Olton Hall is a **commercial property available for private hire**, as well as a popularly-requested display item, **the Hogwarts Express is frequently protected by an Unplottability Spell** and cannot be easily found—unless you know where to look.

> "In May 2009 [Olton Hall] was moved temporarily to the Gloucestershire Warwickshire Railway, and in July 2009 she was based at Tyseley for use on some of the regular 'Shakespeare Express' trains run by Vintage Trains during the Summer. 5972 returned to the G&WR during their annual Wizard's Weekend event in 2010. Late 2011 saw the Loco on static display in Hyde Park, London still in her 'Hogwarts' red livery."

Site Rating

😎 The National Railway Museum is Assigned a Might-be-Fun Rating Because:

• The Olton Hall is not a regular exhibit at either NRM locations. To see this steam locomotive, your Potter Places holiday will have to be planned around dates of a special event that includes exhibition of the Hogwarts Express.

• For various mechanical or commercial reasons, the Olton Hall is sometimes added to, or cancelled from, an NRM special event at the last minute. Happily, when last minute cancellations occur, the NRM website is promptly updated.

• When exhibited, the Olton Hall is usually accompanied by **a set of matched coaching stock** (passenger carriages), also owned by West Coast Railways. You'll be able to *enter* one of the coaches and snap plenty of phenomenal Potter Pix.

• The **York NRM** is at least a 90-minute drive from the nearest Potter Places: **Hardwick Hall** (Site #47), **Malham Cove** (Site #48), **Goathland** (Site #46), or **Durham Cathedral** (Site #45).

Harry Potter Places Book Four

- Although a 2-hour drive from Hardwick Hall or Malham Cove, and a 90-minute drive from Goathland, you can motor from Durham Cathedral to the **Shildon NRM** in only 35 minutes.

- The **Harry Potter WB Studio Tour** (*Harry Potter Places* Book One, London Side-Along Site #27) **does *not* include a full-sized replica of the Hogwarts Express.** Unless you'll be visiting the **Wizarding World of Harry Potter** in Florida, the NRM is probably your only chance to snap Hogwarts Express pix.

We suggest that Potterites with plenty of holiday time check the National Railway Museum's website for Olton Hall's availability. If the Hogwarts Express is unplottable during your visit dates, do not despair! There are plenty of far more convenient Potter Places to enjoy.

Only Potterites who also are **Rail Fans** should schedule an entire vacation around finding and visiting the Hogwarts Express.

Plan Your Visit

Begin by going to the National Railway Museum website and clicking on their **Plan a visit** link. Next, explore the **What's on** links for *both* the York and Shildon locations. If you've recently been dosed with a dollop of **Felix Felicis** (liquid luck), you'll discover an NRM event that includes the Olton Hall steam locomotive on a date for your itinerary.

[Webpage screenshots (enhanced) ©2012 National Railway Museum]

Please Note: Do *not* use the NRM website's Search Engine to seek information about the "Hogwarts Express" or "Olton Hall." In addition to the Unplottability Spell often in effect, locomotive 5972 is occasionally cursed with **Confundus Charms**.

For instance, the webpage screenshot seen above right proclaims that you can **See the Hogwarts Express** at the **NRM Shildon** between 10am and 5pm "**Until early July**." Unfortunately, that webpage fails to identify the **year** of the exhibit's availability. Accessed using the NRM search engine in May of 2012, we were finally able to discover that the advertised exhibit had closed in early July of **2011**.

National Railway Museum—Site 49

[©2012 Tara Bellers]

Another Confundus Conundrum: For some unknown reason, the Olton Hall doesn't bear a *Hogwarts Express* nameplate. Instead, her nameplate reads, the **Wizard Express**. On her side is a destination plate that reads, **Hogwarts Castle**, so the nameplate irregularity isn't due to royalty issues. Whatever the reason, don't be surprised to hear Muggles—or NRM officials—calling her the Wizard Express *or* the Hogwarts Castle.

[©2012 Tara Bellers]

If you cannot find clear mention of the Olton Hall being exhibited during your visit dates, **Email the NRM and ask**. There may be an Olton Hall exhibit in the development stage, or they may know where the Hogwarts Express is appearing during your holiday.

Harry Potter Places Book Four

Operation Hours and Entry Fees

This information is best obtained from the National Railway Museum webpage related to the Olton Hall exhibit you plan to enjoy. While *general* admission to both NRM locations is free, special exhibits are accompanied by special entry fees and times.

Visit Time

Potterites who take the time to visit *either* NRM location should allow at least 2 hours to enjoy the museum.

🛏 Lodging Options

The York or Shildon National Railway Museum is a between-site foray. Explore lodgings at the site you'll reach at the end of your NRM visit day.

Going to the National Railway Museum

The NRM website offers **How to get here** links for both of its locations, whether using public transportation or driving.

🚗 **NRM York SatNav/GPS coordinates:** Leeman Road, York, YO26 4XJ

🚗 **NRM Shildon SatNav/GPS coordinates:** Shildon, Co Durham, DL4 1PQ

Hogwarts Express Potter Pix

The most favorite Hogwarts Express fan pix are *not* screenshot reproductions. They are photos snapped while standing with the Wizard Express nameplate, and the Hogwarts Castle destination plate, in the shot. Additionally, Olton Hall's **tender car** (behind the locomotive) bears a **Hogwarts Railways** sign that includes the **Hogwarts Coat of Arms**.

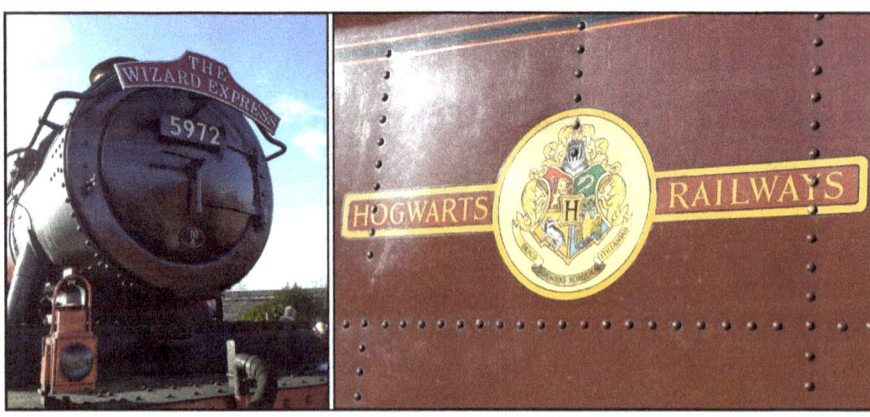

[©2012 Tara Bellers]

National Railway Museum—Site 49

Still, we've included a few screenshots to remind you of other poses you'll enjoy, especially when able to enter one of the carriages.

Hogwarts Express Potter Pic #1

[*Deathly Hallows Part 2* screenshot (enhanced)]

The remaining Potter Pix are all *Sorcerer's Stone* (enhanced) screenshots.

Hogwarts Express Potter Pic #2

Hogwarts Express Potter Pic #3

Harry Potter Places Book Four

Hogwarts Express Potter Pic #4

Hogwarts Express Potter Pic #5

Please Note: Potterites visiting **Scotland** will have the opportunity to take a trip in a Hogwarts-Express-like steam train—the **Jacobite**—and travel over the **Glenfinnan Viaduct**!

[©2009 Tara Bellers, above and below]

National Railway Museum—Site 49

See **Fort William and the West Coast Railway** (Site # 59) in *Harry Potter Places* **Book Five—Scotland: Hogwarts' Home**. There you'll find tips to improve your chances of riding in a Harry-Potter-like compartment, as well as suggestions for enjoying the Muggle Food Trolley.

The End

Thus ends the adventures of
Harry Potter Places Book Four ...

Please join us in Harry Potter Places
Book Five — Scotland: Hogwarts' Home

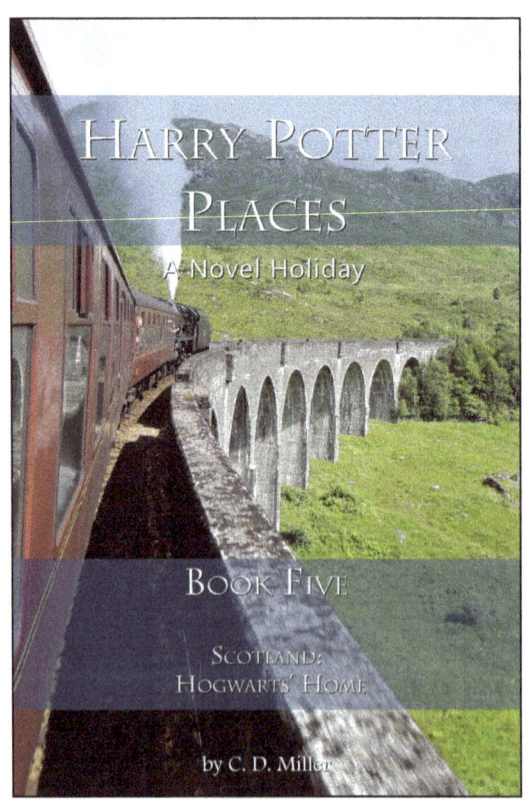

Index

A

Aidensfield 56
Alnwick Castle 15
Alnwick Garden 28
Alnwick Youth Hostel 30

B

Battleaxes to Broomsticks Tours 18
Bellers
   Tara vii, viii, ix
Bess of Hardwick 72
Bloomsbury Publishing Plc. iii
Bramblett
   Reid 8, 10

C

Carson
   Dina C viii
Courtyard Café 19

D

Dale
   Ben viii
   Karen viii

F

Fairhaven Country Guesthouse 67
Fodor's Travel Guides 7
Ford Anglia 105E Deluxe 56
Frommer's Travel Guides 7

G

Glendale House vii, 68
Goathland vii
Goathland Hotel 68

H

Hardwick Garden 75
Hardwick Old Hall 75
Harry Potter Wikia 72
Heartbeat 56
Hilltop Farm Bunk Barn 98
Hogsmead Station 55
Hogwarts Express 103
Hotspur Restaurant 19

I

Inn on The Moor Hotel & Holiday
   Cottages 68

L

Lister Arms Hotel, Restaurant &
   Pub 96
Lonely Planet Guides 7

M

Malfoy Manor 71
Malham National Park Centre 97
Malham Youth Hostel 98
Mallyan Spout Hotel 68
Mletzko
   Wolfgang vii

O

Olton Hall 103

P

Percy Tenantry Volunteers 28
Poison Garden 29
Pottergate Tower 27
Professor McGonagall's Classroom
   37

R

Raincoast Books iii
Regimental Museum of the Royal
    Northumberland Fusiliers 28
Rick Steves' Guidebooks 7
Rough Guides 7
Rowling
  J K iii, 2, 3

S

Scholastic Corporation iii
Simmonds
  Keith vii
  Sandra vii
Smart Traveler Enrollment Program 9
Steves
  Rick 7

T

Talbot
  Elizabeth 72

U

UK Car Rental 11
UK Internet Access 11
UK Photography 11
UK Telephones 11
UK Terminology 11
Undercroft Restaurant 43
University College 51

V

VAT Tax 9
Visit Britain 9

W

Warner Brothers Entertainment, Inc. iii
Wartime Weekend 60
Wikimedia viii
Wikipedia viii

Y

Yorkshire Dales National Park 97

www.ingramcontent.com/pod-product-compliance
Lightning Source LLC
Chambersburg PA
CBHW051945160426
43198CB00013B/2313